LIVING, DYING

Living FOREVER

SPIRITUAL REFLECTIONS ON THE JOURNEY OF LIFE

DR. DAVID SHERBINO

CASTLE QUAY BOOKS

Living, Dying, Living Forever: Spiritual Reflections on the Journey of Life

Copyright ©2014 David Sherbino
All rights reserved
Printed in Canada
International Standard Book Number: 978-1-927355-54-1
ISBN 978-1-927355-55-8 EPUB

Published by:
Castle Quay Books
Pickering, Ontario, L1W 1A5
Tel: (416) 573-3249
E-mail: info@castlequaybooks.com   www.castlequaybooks.com

Edited by Marina H. Hofman Willard
Cover design by Burst Impressions
Printed at Essence Publishing, Belleville, Ontario

Library and Archives Canada Cataloguing in Publication

Sherbino, David, author
Living, dying, living forever : spiritual reflections on the journey of life / Dr. David Sherbino.

Includes bibliographical references.
Issued in print and electronic formats.
ISBN 978-1-927355-54-1 (pbk.).—ISBN 978-1-927355-55-8 (epub)

1. Death—Religious aspects—Christianity. 2. Life—Religious
aspects—Christianity. 3. Christian life. I. Title.

BT825.S54 2014   236'.1   C2014-900668-3
                                        C2014-900669-1

CASTLE QUAY BOOKS

TABLE OF CONTENTS

AUTHOR'S NOTE

In recent years there has been an increased interest in the topic of death and life after death. Most of us know that one day we will die, but at the same time there is a reluctance to talk seriously about the issues we will face. As a minister with years of congregational experience I have witnessed how many people who were dying never had the opportunity to explore the important issues of their life or even to say goodbye, simply because the topic of their death was too painful to address.

Living, Dying, Living Forever is a statement about life. We live, we will die, and we will live beyond death; but in order to die well and to live with the hope of life beyond death, we need to learn to live well. This book is intended to help you explore significant issues in life and to be able to speak to others about your thoughts and wishes so that when the time comes for your death you are able to bring closure and commit yourself to the care of God, with no regrets.

Written from a Christian perspective, the material enables you to explore not only your relationship with God but also your relationship with others—the two things that will last forever. As your relationship with God grows and develops you begin to see life from the perspective that eternal life has already begun and will continue beyond the moment of your death. This is what gives hope, even in the midst of all the struggles and challenges of life. The words of Scripture enable you to have a forward approach to life because you know the best is yet to come.

> *"No eye has seen, no ear has heard, no mind has conceived what God has prepared for those who love him."* (1 Corinthians 2:9)

INTRODUCTION

For everything there is a season, and a time for every matter under heaven: a time to be born, and a time to die; a time to plant, and a time to pluck up…a time to seek, and a time to lose.
(Ecclesiastes 3:1,2,6, NRSV)

These words from Ecclesiastes are familiar to most, yet seldom do we give serious consideration to the implication of this message for our lives. On one level we know there is a time for all of us to die, but at another level we want to keep the topic of death away from our day-to-day experience.

Regularly we are confronted by images of death through news events about accidents, homicides, terrorist attacks, civil wars or natural disasters. We are exposed to images of children dying from disease and famine with appeals to the wider community to assist in any way possible. Perhaps some of you have lost a loved one, and you know the sorrow and heartbreak death brings.

In the Old Testament, death was perceived as a reality that needed to be acknowledged. The Psalmist wrote, "*Teach us to number our days aright, that we may gain a heart of wisdom*" (Psalm 90:12). In a recent course I taught on death and dying, students were asked to take some time to discuss their thoughts about death with family members and what they desired when the time came for them to die. At the end of the semester when the subject was revisited, less than half the class had talked to their family members about dying, and of the half who did many of their family members told them they did not want to pursue the conversation. It was too upsetting to think about dying, and they wanted to avoid discussing the topic, because death is something that is bad.

Granted, most would not see death as something good, but some deaths are perceived as better than others. In the Old Testament a premature death was perceived as a bad death, and even today we speak of people dying too young. The implication is that they have not had the opportunity to experience life to the full. When Hezekiah, the king of Judah, was recovering from his illness, he reflected on dying at such a young age. "*In the prime of my life must I go through the gates of death and be robbed of the rest of my years?*" (Isaiah 38:10).

Death by violence was also considered a bad death. Amos the prophet spoke about Jeroboam, who would die by the sword. Today we still use the words of Jesus: "*All who draw the sword will die by the sword*" (Matthew 26:52). The implication is that those who choose to live a violent life will die a violent death, but we also view any death by violence as horrible.

Lastly, to die without an heir was considered a bad death. The writer of Ecclesiastes tells of a man who had no heir and yet worked all of his life, gaining great wealth. Ultimately it was in vain; there was no one to whom he could pass it on, and he would die alone (Ecclesiastes 4:8).

Absalom, the son of King David, was a man whose life embodied all three aspects of a bad death. He died as a young man, he died a violent death, and he left no heir. On the other hand, to die a good death meant you died in old age, having lived your life to the full; you died in peace and you died with your children and family surrounding you.[1] If you ask people today what constitutes a good death they will say, "Having lived a full life, at peace with everyone, and being surrounded by your loved ones."

These three factors were major concerns about death, but the Old Testament saints had one more concern. They believed death would separate the person from God, and this alone made death so terrible. The prophet Isaiah declared, "*The grave cannot praise you, death cannot sing your praise…The living, the living—they praise you*" (Isaiah 38:18–19). The thought of death filled people with despair since God could not be praised from the grave, but the psalmist introduced a word of hope. He declared, "*God will redeem my life from the grave; he will surely take me to himself*" (Psalm 49:15). In other words, death was not the end of it all, but God would take his own to be with him. Ultimately this hope was fully realized by the resurrection of Jesus, who conquered death and assured his followers that death was not final or the end. Jesus declared, "*I am the resurrection and the life. He who believes in me will live, even though he dies; and whoever lives and believes in me will never die*" (John 11:25–26). God triumphed over death!

We will all die, but in order to die well we need to learn to live well. John Henry Cardinal Newman once stated, "Fear not that your life will come to an end, but rather that it will never have had a beginning."

In medieval times Christians thought about their death. Disease that brought about death was rampant, and daily the death toll rose. The awareness of their impending death caused many to prepare for it through what was termed *ars moriendi* (the art of dying).[2] This was a series of instructions on how to prepare for one's death, and death was seen as a spiritual event that was to be actively undertaken in the light of eternity.

In many respects the life we are living is a prelude and preparation for the life to come. The psychologist Theresa Rando suggests that knowing we will die one day helps us to live differently: we will savour life; we will find new strength to make major decisions; it will reveal the importance of intimacy and to see our achievements as having had significance.[3] All this may be true, but from a Christian perspective there is much more.

If we are going to live forever in eternity with God, then first and foremost we need to consider our relationship with God. One day we will step through the doorway of death and stand face to face with God. Knowing this, it is essential we grow in our relationship with God. We need to be focused on developing a deeper intimacy with the One who created us and who called us to be his children. Therefore we need to ask, "Do I love God more and more day by day? Is there anything that is taking his rightful place in my life? Is there anything that is causing me to drift away from him?"

We need to anticipate that along the way there will be challenges and difficulties that can cause us to lose focus. We may drift away from God, or we may find that these troublesome times are really opportunities to learn to depend on him for more and more of his strength. Author Ken Boa writes,

> Far from promising a life of ease and prosperity, the New Testament affirms that those who follow Christ will face a new dimension of obstacles and struggles that they did not know before they committed their lives to him. In fact, the intensity of spiritual warfare is proportional to the seriousness of a believer's response to the terms of discipleship...At the end of his last discourse to his disciples, Jesus assured them "These things I have spoken to you, so that in me you may have peace. In this world you will have tribulation, but take courage! I have overcome the world" (John 16:33).[4]

Living, Dying, Living Forever

This workbook is designed to help you explore a number of issues that relate to your life and your relationship with God. In our living and in our dying we need to be assured daily of the grace and love of God. *Living, Dying, Living Forever* is a spiritual experience that will enable you to consider how to live differently in order that you may die well and have the assurance of living forever. You need to be able to sort out issues that will make the journey exciting and hopeful.

Take your time, explore the issues raised, ask God to give you the insight and wisdom you need, and then act on whatever he tells you to do. God will empower you to take the right steps. You may want to quit; persevere. You are on a journey, and when this phase of eternal life is completed, God will call you home, and you will see him face to face.

Prayer

> *To him who is able to keep you from falling and to present you before his glorious presence without fault and with great joy—to the only God our Savior be glory, majesty, power and authority, through Jesus Christ our Lord, before all ages, now and forevermore! Amen.* (Jude 1:24–25)

CHAPTER ONE
THE JOURNEY

Let us run with perseverance the race marked out for us. Let us fix our eyes on Jesus.
(Hebrews 12:1–2)

Blessing on the Journey

> May the road rise to meet you.
> May the wind be always at your back.
> May the sun shine warm upon your face
> And the rains fall softly upon your fields.
> And until we meet again
> May God hold you in the palm of his hand.
> (Irish Blessing)

If you were told you had a limited amount of time to live, how would this influence the way you lived out your remaining days? Would your values change? Would you make radical changes, or would you continue living as you presently do?

There are some people who would make radical changes and try to accomplish their goals in the time they have left. The movie *The Bucket List,* starring Jack Nicholson as a hedonistic multimillionaire and Morgan Freeman as a loyal married mechanic, is about two men stricken with cancer who wind up as roommates in the hospital and eventually become friends. When their prognoses turn grim, they make an agreement to complete a "bucket list," an inventory of things they want to do before they die—or "kick the bucket." They make a plan, but the plan is not as a simple as they anticipated. Both have unfinished business, but the biggest challenge they discover is being able to face death knowing they have made peace with their lives.

Living, Dying, Living Forever

Many people, especially those who are young, want to deny the imminence of death. On the one hand, all of us know we will ultimately die, but we hope it is somewhere in the distant future. On the other hand, the Bible emphasizes the brevity of life and the need to invest our lives wisely. David the Psalmist wrote,

> *"Show me, O LORD, my life's end and the number of my days; let me know how fleeting is my life. You have made my days a mere hand-breadth; the span of my years is as nothing before you. Each man's life is but a breath…Man is a mere phantom as he goes to and fro: He bustles about, but only in vain; he heaps up wealth, not knowing who will get it. But now, Lord, what do I look for? My hope is in you."* (Psalm 39:4–7)

The prophet Isaiah contrasted the temporal and the eternal with a different metaphor:

> *"All men are like grass, and all their glory is like the flowers of the field. The grass withers and the flowers fall, because the breath of the LORD blows on them. Surely the people are grass. The grass withers and the flowers fall, but the word of our God stands forever."* (Isaiah 40:6–8)

These writers are telling us that life is shorter than most of us realize and it is important that we live wisely. It is not uncommon to hear older people say, "Life goes by so quickly," but younger people do not seem to grasp this concept. For them, time seems like eternity. It's all about perspective. For example, two weeks on a diet seems to be much longer than two weeks on vacation. The prophet Isaiah declared that the years of our lives, from the perspective of generations that have come and gone, are no longer than the duration of a flower in the field (Isaiah 40:6–8). In other words, life is really short!

At first glance this seems to be so pessimistic, and all we can hope for is living life to the full and making sure we complete our "bucket lists." Ken Boa of Reflection Ministries offers a different perspective to these words of Isaiah. He writes,

> It comes as no surprise to see this perspective as realistic, but it is surprising to discover that it is also hopeful. It is hopeful precisely because it informs us that there is more to life than what we presently see, and it assures us that our longing for more that this world can offer is not merely a pipe dream. The biblical vision of God's invitation to us is not only forgiveness, but newness of life in Christ, a new quality of relational life that will never fade or tarnish.[5]

However, for many, their focus is on the temporal and not the eternal, as we have bought into the concept that everything is in the here and now. The movie *Dead Poets Society,* set in New England during the 1950s at Welton Academy, is about an English teacher, John Keating, portrayed by Robin Williams, who seeks to communicate to his students that you can't gain all the wisdom you need in a few years. In one scene he takes his young idealistic students to view the photo gallery of past alumni. The people in the photos were once like these ambitious young men, but now they are all dead. Then Keating whispers into the ears of the students the memorable words *Carpe diem* (seize the day). Sadly, many try to invest their lives in much that will not last, and each day is more of the same. The journey of life is travelled at a frantic pace, and we try to cram into each day as much as we can before the funeral director arrives and picks us up. In this pursuit of life many have never asked if this will give them the meaning and satisfaction they are searching for. Alice, in the book *Alice in Wonderland,* asks the Cheshire cat, "Would you tell me, please, which way I ought to go from here?" "That depends a good deal on where you want to get to," says the Cat. "I don't much care where," says Alice. "Then it doesn't much matter which way you go," says the Cat. Reflecting on this statement, Boa comments,

> If we have not decided where we are going, one road will do as well or as poorly as another. The problem is that the outcome of the unexamined life is rarely satisfactory. If we fail to pursue God's purpose for our lives, we are likely to suffer from destination sickness, the discovery that when we reach our destination, it's not all it was cracked up to be.[6]

So what is your journey like? Have you ever thought about your final destination? In the Bible there are many depictions of life as a journey. In the Old Testament, there is the story of the journey of the Israelites from the exodus out of Egypt, 40 years of wandering in the wilderness and eventually reaching the Promised Land. In the New Testament, many are familiar with the three missionary journeys of the apostle Paul as he travelled throughout Asia Minor, bringing the good news of the gospel to many people.

As God led the children of Israel out of the bondage and slavery in Egypt to the Promised Land of freedom, so the Christian life as depicted in the New Testament is one of deliverance from the slavery and bondage of sin into the freedom we have in Christ.

The apostle Paul spoke of this journey as a race. In life, he tells us, there will be many demands, obstacles and difficulties, but we are not to be discouraged. In fact, he urges us to press on, because when we do we will receive the prize at the end of the race. At the end of his life Paul would write that he had completed the race.

> *I have fought the good fight. I have finished the race, I have kept the faith. Now there is in store for me the crown of righteousness, which the Lord, the righteous Judge, will award to me on that day—and not only to me, but also to all who have longed for his appearing* (2 Timothy 4:7–8).

Living, Dying, Living Forever

The writer to the Hebrews urges the readers to persevere. Journeys are not always easy. The Israelites while on their forty-year trek experienced many difficulties and challenges. As they reached the edge of the Promised Land, they faced another obstacle—they had to cross the Jordan River. Joshua, the successor of Moses, had been with Moses through thick and thin. He knew the valley of defeat and the mountaintop of success. He also knew that the people were depleted after so many years of wandering and waiting to get to the Promised Land. So what does he say to these people as they face one more challenge? His words are direct, but they are filled with hope. *"Consecrate yourselves, for tomorrow the LORD will do wonders among you"* (Joshua 3:5, ESV). To consecrate themselves meant they were to be totally committed to the Lord. They were to cut themselves off from anything in the past that would hinder their absolute devotion and commitment. That's what we need in our journey. The writer to the Hebrews urges us to

> *Throw off everything that hinders and the sin that so easily entangles, and let us run with perseverance the race marked out for us. Let us fix our eyes on Jesus, the author and perfecter of our faith, who for the joy set before him endured the cross, scorning its shame, and sat down at the right hand of the throne of God.* (Hebrews 12:1–2)

The race is demanding and sometimes agonizing, and it requires determination and perseverance. In the 1600s, while imprisoned for his opposition to the religious policies of King Charles II, John Bunyan wrote the famous book *Pilgrim's Progress.* The story, framed as a dream, is about Christian and his journey from the City of Destruction to the Celestial City, heaven. The story tells of the temptations and struggles Christian faced on this journey of life, but the greatest encouragement that kept him going was the anticipation of his arrival at his destination.

We are challenged to keep going. There are many who have gone on before us, and their stories of faith become an encouragement to keep running the race. We also need to get rid of the sin that can hinder us. The sin that can hinder us is the sin of unbelief, which is when we doubt the promises of God. When we doubt the promises of God we choose to not follow him, because we assume he is not trustworthy. If we choose to trust him, then the most important thing we can do is to keep our eyes fixed on him. He is our example of living by faith. Along the journey, Jesus was tempted and faced numerous challenges, but he always stayed the course, because he would not be distracted and he trusted the Father completely. He finished the race!

As you look at your life, do you focus only on the temporal or do you have the perspective of eternity? All of us are on a journey. What is your destination? Will you arrive safely? Will you stay the course? Every day is an opportunity to stay focused and to keep the goal in mind as you take the next step.

Reflections

1. Take some time to think about your journey of life. What are some of the milestones?

Age 0–6

_____

_____

Age 7–13

_____

_____

Age 14–21

_____

_____

Age 22–40

_____

_____

Age 41–65

_____

_____

Age 70

_____

_____

As you think of these different periods of life, what do you see as important?

_____

_____

_____

2. Who are the significant people who have been an encouragement or mentor to you during your life? What did they do that was so significant to help or encourage you?

_____

_____

_____

3. What is the ultimate destination of your journey? Is there more to life than the here and now? What do you need to change in your life to ensure that you reach your destination?

_____

_____

_____

_____

4. Meditate on these words: "*Show me, O LORD, my life's end and the number of my days; let me know how fleeting is my life*" (Psalm 39:4).

5. If you have a "bucket list," what is one thing you could do now?

_____

_____

_____

6. Prayer:

Lord, in my journey of life may I follow you wherever you lead me. Help me to trust you always and to enjoy each day in your presence. I am grateful that you are with me always and in the end you will receive me unto yourself. You alone are my hope and my destiny.
Amen.

CHAPTER TWO
GETTING CLOSER TO GOD

Love the Lᴏʀᴅ your God with all your heart and with all your soul and with all your strength.
(Deuteronomy 6:5)

A life of intimacy with God is characterized by joy.
(Oswald Chambers)

When God created the first person, what distinguished him from the rest of creation was that he was created in the image of God. In other words, he had the capacity to connect with God and to reflect God's presence in the world. Thus we have the ability to know, to love and to honour the Lord of heaven and earth.

This reality is revealed in the story of Adam and Eve. When God created them to live in the Garden of Eden, they had a wonderful relationship with God, with each other and with the created order around them. God told them that everything was there for their use and enjoyment, but the tree in the centre of the garden they were not to touch. Daily they enjoyed communion with God, until that fateful day when they took and ate of the forbidden fruit.

That evening the couple heard the sound of the Lord God as he was walking in the garden, and they hid from the presence of God. God called out, "Where are you?" It was not a question about their physical location but about their relationship with God. They were designed for intimacy with God, but now they were hiding from God. Hiding from God has been the stance of humanity from that time until the present. God desires to be in relationship with us, but we are living apart from God, and when that happens we discover how lonely and meaningless life can be.

The writer of Ecclesiastes, sometimes referred to as the philosopher, expressed his disillusionment about life. He wrote,

> *I denied myself nothing my eyes desired; I refused my heart no pleasure. My heart took delight in all my work, and this was the reward for all my labor. Yet when I surveyed all that my hands had done and what I had toiled to achieve, everything was meaningless, a chasing after the wind; nothing was gained under the sun.* (Ecclesiastes 2:10–11)

It is obvious that the writer is frustrated. He did not find satisfaction through intellectual pursuits, pleasures or projects he undertook and completed. No matter what we do, there remains a deep longing within each person to know God intimately, and without this there will be a deep dissatisfaction and disconnect.

In Luke 15, Jesus told a story that is somewhat reflective of our story. There was a man who had two sons, and the younger of the two asked his father to give him the portion of the family estate that belonged to him. In that culture, when there were two heirs the eldest received two-thirds and the youngest received the remaining one-third. However, the division of the estate only occurred after the death of the father. So what the young man was actually saying was he wished his dad was dead. The estate meant more to him than the relationship he had with his father.

The father, without hesitation, granted the son's request and the freedom to do as he desired. The younger son went off to a distant land and spent everything he had on a lifestyle he thought would bring him enjoyment. One day he discovered he had nothing. He had no friends, no money, and no dignity. In fact, he was hungry, lonely, trying to survive by working on a pig farm. It was at this point that he came to his senses and thought about returning home. His plan was simple: he would admit he was wrong in what he had done and would ask his father to receive him as a hired hand.

As he makes his way home his father sees him coming, jumps up and runs toward his son, not the typical action of a Middle Eastern father. When they meet he embraces his son and kisses him, for his heart is filled with joy. The young man tries to tell his dad his plan but is interrupted as the father tells the servants to bring shoes and a robe and to prepare a feast. His son has come home.

Meanwhile, the elder brother working in the fields hears the commotion, is curious and inquires as to what is going on. When he learns his young brother has returned home, he refuses to join the celebration and actually chastises his father for welcoming this son home. The elder son is bitter; he works hard for his father, never causes a moment of concern, yet this brother of his who has squandered his resources (and he assumes it was squandered on prostitutes) is given a celebration. He, on the other hand, the good and loyal son, never experiences anything like this, so he is not about to celebrate and enter the joy of his father for a son who had been perceived as dead but is now home safe and sound.

When Jesus told this story there were two audiences listening to him. The author Tim Keller comments,

> First there were the "tax collectors and sinners." These men and women correspond to the younger brother. They observed neither the moral laws of the Bible nor the rules for ceremonial purity followed by the religious Jews. They engaged in "wild living." Like the younger brother, they "left home" by leaving the traditional morality of their families and of respectable society. The second group of listeners was the "Pharisees and the teachers of the law," who were represented by the elder brother. They held to the traditional morality of their upbringing. They studied and obeyed the Scripture. They worshipped faithfully and prayed constantly."[7]

Obviously the younger brother used his father to get what he wanted, and the elder brother obeyed his father to get what he wanted. Some, who are in the category of the elder brother, believe their performance gives them status with the father. They can say and do all the right things, but their heart is "in the far country." In reality, both brothers are lost and alone.

The author Joseph Stowell defines aloneness as

> What we feel when we are functionally disconnected at the core of our being from all that truly satisfies, sustains, and secures. It is the absence of an experiential sense of God's presence, power, and pleasure to supply us with the resources that support all of life. It is the ultimate consequence of trusting in companions and commodities that are, at the end of the day, insufficient.[8]

The opposite of aloneness, according to Stowell, is intimacy, and there is nothing else in the entire world that can meet this deep longing of the heart. However, he believes that true intimacy is only found "in a growing relationship to the One who is perfectly suited to satisfy us and sustain us…intimacy is what we experience as we grow more deeply conscious of, connected to, and confident in him and him alone as our unfailing resource in life."[9] Sadly, only the younger son would discover that relationship.

This account is often referred to as "The Story of the Prodigal Son." The term "prodigal" means "extravagant," and in one sense the younger son was prodigal in that he lived an extravagant lifestyle, hoping that it would give him meaning or purpose or at least some moments of happiness. I am convinced that the story should be called "The Prodigal Father," because the father was absolutely extravagant in his love for both of his sons. This is what we need in all relationships, including our relationship with God—extravagant love.

The Pharisees asked Jesus what was the greatest commandment. He replied, "*Love the Lord your God with all your heart and with all your soul and with all your mind and with all your strength*" (Mark 12:30). This implies loving God with the totality of our being. It is a lived experience and not an intellectual exercise. Paul declared, "*I want to know Christ*" (Philippians 3:10). This implies he wanted to experience Christ in every aspect of life.

The second commandment Jesus spoke about was "*Love your neighbor as yourself*" (Mark 12:31). Our love for God will always be expressed in our relationships with others.

As we consider God's love for us, it ought to leave us breathless. His love is spontaneous and unending, and he chose to love us simply because he chose to love us. There are some who accept this as a theological truth but have not yet experienced it nor internalized it. Richard of Chichester in the 13th century wrote a prayer, popularized in the song "Day by Day," that expresses three factors to help us grow closer to God:

> Thanks be to you, O Lord Jesus Christ,
> for all the benefits which you have given us;
> for all the pains and insults which you have borne for us.
> O most merciful Redeemer, Friend, and Brother,
> may we know you more clearly,
> love you more dearly,
> and follow you more nearly;
> for your own sake.

The first aspect of the prayer is to know God more clearly. This is much more than propositional truth. The apostle Paul's prayer for the Christians in Ephesus was "*that the eyes of your heart may be enlightened in order that you may know the hope to which he has called you, the riches of his glorious inheritance in the saints, and his incomparably great power for us who believe*" (Ephesians 1:18–19).

The question remains, what do we need to do to know God more clearly? The author Ken Boa believes,

> The two essential ingredients are time and obedience. It takes time to cultivate a relationship, and unless we set aside consistent time for solitude, silence, prayer, and Scripture reading, we will never become intimate with our Lord. Obedience is the proper response to this communication, since it is our personal expression of trust in the promises of the Person we are coming to know.[10]

Jesus said very clearly, "*If you love me, you will obey my commandments*" (John 14:15, GWT).

There will be those who wonder who has the time for this type of a relationship when our lives are consumed with busyness. In fact, many find their identity and measure their worth by what they do and how much they accomplish. Biblical scholar Bruce Demarest comments,

> Nourishing the inner man comes through relationship (being). The inner man is drained as the result of compulsion (legalism) and hyperactivity (doing). The life empowered to obey God only flows from a heart relationship with him, in the manner of Christ. With this in mind, we can understand Jesus' words: "yes I am the vine; you are the branches. Those who remain in me, and I in them, will produce much fruit. For apart from me you can do nothing" (John 15:5). Only as we are graced with God's peaceful presence are we really equipped to serve him.[11]

The second aspect of the prayer is to love God more dearly. The more we understand what God has done for us, the more our hearts will overflow with love toward him. John wrote, "*We love because he first loved us*" (1 John 4:19). With the father in the story of the two sons, the love given was unmerited and undeserved. So it is with God. As we know him more we love him more.

The final aspect of the prayer is that we would follow him more nearly. Following God is based upon trusting him completely. Even if he asks us to follow him through a challenging and difficult situation, we know that he only has our greater good in mind. Boa states, "Obedience to Christ is the way we test and express our abiding relationship with him."[12]

As we continue this journey it is essential that we develop a growing relationship with the God of heaven and earth, the One who made us for a relationship with himself and who has revealed himself in the person of Jesus Christ. Whether you perceive yourself as the younger brother or the older brother, the message is the same: God desires an intimate relationship with you.

The theologian James Packer declares,

> What matters most supremely, therefore, is not, in the last analysis, the fact that I know God, but the larger fact that underlies it—the fact that he knows me. I am graven on the palms of his hands; I am never out of his mind. All knowledge of him depends on his sustained initiative in knowing me. I know him because he first knew me and continues to know me. He knows me as friend. There is tremendous relief in knowing that his love for me is utterly realistic based at every point on prior knowledge of the worst about me, so that no discovery can now disillusion him about me.[13]

Reflections

1. Take some time to reflect on the story of the prodigal son. Which son do you most clearly identify with? In what sense are you living "in the far country"? (Remember, you can be "in the far country" while still living at home.)

_____

_____

_____

_____

2. Think about the love the father had for both sons. Now meditate on the love you have experienced from your Heavenly Father.

_____

_____

_____

3. What steps can you take to develop a closer relationship with God?

_____

_____

_____

_____

4. Read and reflect on this prayer:

I pray that out of his glorious riches he may strengthen you with power through his Spirit in your inner being, so that Christ may dwell in your hearts through faith. And I pray that you, being rooted and established in love, may have power, together with all the saints, to grasp how wide and long and high and deep is the love of Christ, and to know this love that surpasses knowledge—that you may be filled to the measure of all the fullness of God. (Ephesians 3:16–19)

CHAPTER THREE
LETTING GO OF THE PAST

"I am the Lord's servant…
May it be to me as you have said."
(Luke 1:38)

How different our lives are when we really know what is deeply important to us, and keeping that picture in mind, we manage ourselves each day to be and to do what really matters most.
(Stephen Covey)

Some things in life are difficult to let go of because most of us like to be in control. When we are in control of situations we have a feeling of security and confidence. However, there are situations in life we cannot control, and we must let go. It may be plans we have made, it may involve releasing our children as they get older or relinquishing some of our possessions, and for everyone it will involve letting go of life as we face our death.

Have you ever noticed how difficult it is to let go of some things? Try going for an entire day without checking your email or responding to a text message or using your cellphone. In a recent Zoomer study of Canadians 45 and older, 76 percent said they would rather give up anything than their Internet-enabled device. Perhaps some are going into withdrawal just contemplating such an idea.

Here is a simple exercise to help you grasp the concept of letting go. Take a small object, perhaps a coin; place it in your hand and clench your fist around it. Hold it tight until your knuckles are white. Some people seem to live life this way. We make statements such as "I am trying to hold on" or "I am struggling to get a grip." Life is perceived as a struggle, and we desperately try to be in control to make things work according to our plans.

Now slowly open your clenched fist and feel the relief as you allow the blood to flow back into your fingers. In the life of faith, when we learn to let go, when we no longer struggle, we discover a sense of peace and calmness.

In the Bible there are stories of people who let go. One of the key Old Testament figures was Job, who at the beginning of his life seemed to have everything. He was described as blameless and upright, a man who loved God and shunned evil. In addition he was a wealthy farmer with numerous herds, and servants to look after them. In fact he was regarded as the wealthiest man in the East. He had a wonderful family, and his children were the love of his life. One day Satan told God that the only reason Job loved and feared God was because his life was going so well. There are people who can claim to have faith and speak about trusting God when things are positive, but when things are not going as planned is when their faith and trust in God is put to the test.

Job lost everything. His animals were stolen, his servants were killed, and a great storm caused the roof of the house where his children were staying to collapse, and they all died. Then Job became very ill. Seeing the terrible things that had happened—natural disaster, illness, death and destruction—all that Job's wife could say to him was *"Curse God and die!"* (Job 2:9). Through all of this Job relinquished control and declared, "*Though he slay me, yet will I hope in him*" (Job 13:15).

Author Richard Foster refers to this act of letting go as a prayer of relinquishment. He writes, "This is the kind of searching prayer that should permeate our entire life experience. In the prayer of relinquishment, we are committed to letting go of our will whenever it conflicts with the will and way of God."[14]

Mary was a young woman whose life plans were radically changed. She and Joseph were engaged to be married. Like most young couples they had plans for their future that may have included building a home, having children and growing old together. All of their plans were radically altered when the angel Gabriel visited Mary and told her that she had found favour with God and had been chosen to be the mother of the Messiah. Furthermore, the child she would bear had been conceived by the Holy Spirit.

This was not the way things ordinarily happened. As Mary thought about this, she realized life would be radically altered. What would Joseph think? What would her parents say? How would the small community where she lived react to this? It was an incredible challenge for a young woman to face. However, as Mary contemplated everything the angel said, she made a decision to trust God. She declared, "*I am the Lord's servant...May it be to me as you have said*" (Luke 1:38). This was Mary's prayer of relinquishment. No matter the cost, Mary was willing to let go of all her plans and surrender herself to the will of God.

The most profound example of "letting go" was evident in life of Jesus. It began with the incarnation and continued through to his death. Jesus left the glory of heaven, came to earth as a baby, grew up as a young man, became the servant of all and ultimately died on a cross. The apostle Paul expressed it in this manner:

> *[Jesus], being in very nature God, did not consider equality with God something to be grasped, but made himself nothing, taking the very nature of a servant, being made in human likeness. And being found in appearance as a man, he humbled himself and became obedient to death—even death on a cross!* (Philippians 2:6–8)

Jesus Christ, the Son of God, who lived in the place of ultimate glory and beauty, voluntarily left it all. He had equality with the Father but chose to empty himself of his deity so that he might identify himself with us and ultimately take our condemnation. This act cost him his life as he went to the cross to make atonement for our sins. It meant letting go.

At the end of his life Jesus would let go again. Prior to his arrest, judgment and crucifixion, Jesus went to the garden of Gethsemane to pray. Knowing what was ahead, he fervently asked his heavenly Father to find some other way. His prayer is a prayer everyone needs to learn if they are to surrender their lives into the hands of God. Translator J. B. Phillips brings the prayer into focus: "*Dear Father...all things are possible to you. Please—let me not have to drink this cup! Yet it is not what I want but what you want*" (Mark 14:36). Richard Foster comments,

> Here we have the incarnate Son praying through his tears and not receiving what he asks. Jesus knew the burden of unanswered prayer. He really did want the cup to pass, and he asked that it would pass. "If you are willing" was his questioning, his wondering. The Father's will was not absolutely clear to him. "Is there any other way?" "Can people be redeemed by some different means?" The answer—no![15]

This prayer of relinquishment by Jesus in the Garden of Gethsemane is a pattern for us. He could have avoided the cross. He could have compromised with the priests, bargained with the high priest. Pilate wanted to release him and tried to get Jesus to say the correct words so that this innocent man could go free. In the garden on the night of his betrayal Jesus had enough time to run from the soldiers. However, he used his free will to turn the decision over to his Father and declared, "Yet not my will but yours." Foster describes this prayer of Jesus as "grace-filled releasing of our will and a flowing into the will of the Father."[16]

These stories give us some insight into letting go. In all of these incidents, letting go was not easy. Job did not understand what was happening to him. He believed, as was the norm of the day, that if you lived a godly life you would be blessed by God. Job did experience many blessings, so when everything changed, he did not know why. He examined his life to see if he had sinned against God but could find no sin. It just did not make sense. He had two choices, curse God or trust God. He chose to trust.

Mary wondered about the message of the angel and was somewhat puzzled. How could she, a virgin, bear the Son of God? As she pondered all these things, she came to the decision that she would do exactly as God asked, and she chose to trust.

Jesus repeatedly asked the Father to remove the cup. This was an issue he wrestled with for the entire night, and in the end he too chose to trust. Letting go and trusting is not easy; in fact, Job, Mary and Jesus discovered it is a struggle. In essence the struggle is "my will versus God's will."

We need to understand that the prayer of relinquishment is not one of resigning ourselves to fate but rather an act of acceptance. The late Catherine Marshall wrote,

> There is a crucial difference between acceptance and resignation. There is no resignation in the prayer of relinquishment. Resignation says, "This is my situation and I must resign myself and settle down to it." Resignation lies down in the dust of a godless universe and steels itself for the worst. Acceptance says "True, this is my situation at the moment. I'll look unblinkingly at it. But I'll also open up my hands to accept willingly whatever a loving heavenly Father sends." Thus acceptance never slams shut the door of hope.[17]

As we learn to trust, hope emerges. Richard Foster writes,

> Even when all we see are the tangled threads on the backside of life's tapestry, we know that God is good and is out to do us good always. That gives us hope to believe that we are the winners, regardless of

what we are being called to relinquish. God is inviting us deeper in and higher up. There is training in righteousness, transforming power, new joys, and deeper intimacy.[18]

Because Jesus was willing to give up what he wanted so that the will of the Father could be done, he now lives to enable us to give up our will and do the will of the Father. The Bible states, "*It is God who works in you to will and to act according to his good purpose*" (Philippians 2:13). When we commit our lives to Christ, our lives belong to him. The apostle Paul expressed it in these words: "*I no longer live, but Christ lives in me*" (Galatians 2:20). Such an act of commitment means we only seek to do the will of the One to whom we belong.

Is God calling you to let go?

It may be your plans, your hopes or your dreams that will not be fulfilled in the manner you thought. Are you willing to submit your will to the will of the One who loves you and will give you the very best? If you do, this is your act of relinquishment.

Reflections

1. What is difficult for you to relinquish? Take some time to write down the issues that come to mind.

2. From your list take one item at a time and offer it to God. Perhaps you need to write out a prayer that encompasses this act of letting go.

3. Imagine you are near the end of your life, or perhaps you are there now. What do you need to let go? Can you release this to God and trust him to meet all your needs?

4. Memorize this verse: "*God will meet all your needs according to his glorious riches in Christ Jesus*" (Philippians 4:19).

5. Read the Prayer of Relinquishment and take some time to meditate on the words:

Relinquishment

Father, I abandon myself into your hands.
Do with me whatever you will.
Whatever you may do, I thank you.
I am ready for all, I accept all.
Let only your will be done in me,
and in all your creatures.
Into your hands I commend my spirit.
I offer it to you with all the love that is in my heart.
For I love you, Lord, and so want to give myself,
To surrender myself into your hands,
without reserve and with boundless confidence,
for you are my Father.
Amen.
(Charles de Foucauld)

A Prayer of Relinquishment

Today, O Lord, I yield myself to you.
May your will be my delight throughout the day.
May your love be the pattern of my living.
I surrender to you my hopes, my dreams, my ambitions.
Do with them what you will, when you will, as you will.
I place into your loving care my family, friends and my future.
I release into your hands my need to control, my craving for status, my fear of obscurity.
Eradicate all evil, purify the good.
Establish your kingdom on earth.
For Jesus' sake.
Amen.
(Anonymous)

CHAPTER FOUR
LOOKING FORWARD

Forgetting what is behind…
I press on toward the goal to win
the prize for which God has called
me heavenward in Christ Jesus.
(Philippians 3:13–14)

Life can only be understood
backwards, but it must be lived
forwards.
(Soren Kierkegaard)[19]

A lot of people live in the past, and at times we hear them say, "what if" or "if only." Others simply reminisce and fail to look to the future and all that lies ahead.

If we allow the past to be the present focus of our life, we simply live out our days reminiscing or moaning about our failures or lost opportunities, and we never look forward to the new opportunities and challenges that are before us. Steven Jobs at 30 years of age was fired from Apple. In 2005, he spoke of this experience at the commencement at Stanford University. This is what he said to these young graduates as they embarked on their future:

I didn't see it then, but it turned out that getting fired from Apple was the best thing that could have ever happened to me. The heaviness of being successful was replaced by the lightness of being a beginner again, less sure about everything. It freed me to enter one of the most creative periods of my life...When I was 17, I read a quote that went something like: "If you live each day as if it was your last, someday you'll most certainly be right." It made an impression on me, and since then, for the past 33 years, I have looked in the mirror every morning and asked myself: "If today were the last day of my life, would I want to do what I am about to do today?" And whenever the answer has been "No" for too many days in a row, I know I need to change something. Remembering that I'll be dead soon is the most important tool I've ever encountered to help me make the big choices in life. Because almost everything—all external expectations, all pride, all fear of embarrassment or failure—these things just fall away in the face of death, leaving only what is truly important.[20]

How often have you said, "what if" or "if only"? We may have regrets about decisions we have made and how the outcome negatively affected our life, or perhaps we never took risks and simply lived life in the "safe zone." Now we wonder what would have happened "if only I had..." or "what if" circumstances were different—would I have made other decisions?

Living in the present is about the here and now, making the most of the situations you find yourself in. Living in the future is about planning for your tomorrows, seeing the path your life is on and evaluating its direction to determine if it is going to give your life the meaning you want or desire.

Are you living in the past, bemoaning lost opportunities, or are you choosing to live each day to the fullest with your eye on the future?

The apostle Paul was a forward-living person. He wrote,

Not that I...have already been made perfect, but I press on to take hold of that for which Christ Jesus took hold of me. Brothers, I do not consider myself yet to have taken hold of it. But one thing I do: Forgetting what is behind and straining toward what is ahead, I press on toward the goal to win the prize for which God has called me heavenward in Christ Jesus. (Philippians 3:12–14)

Paul chose to live each day with his eye toward the future because he saw that life was about "one thing." Imagine being so focused that there is only one thing that really matters, and it is the driving force of your life. Most have so many competing loyalties that life is not focused but fragmented and scattered, and consequently we are pulled in many different directions. Imagine being able to say like Paul *"one thing I do."*

In the Old Testament there is an amazing story of a young Jewish woman named Esther. Her life was about "one thing." At the time of Esther the Jews were living in exile in Persia. The ruler, King Xerxes, wanted to display his wife before all his guests at a prestigious banquet he was giving. The queen refused to be treated as an object of display, and as a result the king in anger had her removed from his presence forever. A search to replace the queen was conducted, and it concluded when the king was attracted to the young Jewish woman Esther and crowned her queen.

Now Esther had been raised by her uncle, Mordecai, who told her to keep her family background and nationality a secret. One of the royal officials, a man called Haman, was not only a high ranking official in the government but also close to the king. This man loved to be acknowledged by the masses, and he expected everyone to bow before him whenever he went out in public. One man, a Jew named Mordecai, refused to bow or pay him honour. This infuriated Haman to such a degree that he devised a plot to exterminate all the Jews in the entire kingdom of Xerxes. He had the king issue an edict that stated they were to *"kill and annihilate all the Jews—young and old, women and little children—on a single day, the thirteenth day of the twelfth month, the month of Adar, and to plunder their goods"* (Esther 3:13). All the Jews were in great distress and turmoil.

Mordecai, Esther's uncle, approached her and told her she was the one hope for the entire nation. Only she could change the mind of the king. In fact, even though she was the queen, her life would not be spared, because she too was Jewish! Then Mordecai spoke to Esther words that have resonated throughout the centuries: *"Who knows but that you have come to royal position for such a time as this?"* (Esther 4:14). Esther was challenged by Mordecai's words and replied, *"I will go to the king, even though it is against the law. And if I perish, I perish"* (Esther 4:16). Suddenly her life became focused; it was all about one thing—saving a nation!

Most are not called to save a nation, but like the apostle Paul our life can become so focused that we can say, "One thing I do!" To be able to do this we will need to discover what is really important, and to do that we may have to get rid of some baggage we carry around from the past.

Paul said he needed to forget the past. What was there about his past that could hinder his moving forward? First, he had his reputation. He was an ardent Jew; he kept all the requirements of the law, and he was zealous in his persecution of the church. He consented to the stoning of Stephen, the first Christian martyr, and he was involved in the rounding up and incarceration of the followers of Jesus. Could he let go of these memories of the terrible things he did in his past, or would they remain etched forever in his mind, constantly reminding him that he had been a zealous but misguided religious fanatic?

There were others aspects of his life that he would need to let go. When he became a follower of Jesus he discovered many other challenges that could have had a negative effect on him and easily become the focus of his life. Paul summarized his life experiences:

> What anyone else dares to boast about—I am speaking as a fool—I also dare to boast about. Are they Hebrews? So am I. Are they Israelites? So am I. Are they Abraham's descendants? So am I. Are they servants of Christ? (I am out of my mind to talk like this.) I am more. I have worked much harder, been in prison more frequently, been flogged more severely, and been exposed to death again and again. (2 Corinthians 11:21–23)

Paul knew there were some who were envious of him and the success he had in establishing churches though out Asia Minor. Knowing himself as he did, it would have been easy for Paul to assume that he was more committed to the cause of Christ than anyone else. He had to let all of this go if he was to do "one thing" and not allow pride to control his life.

Jeremy Lin of the New York Nicks had to focus on one thing. Eryn Sun of Christian Post tells how Lin struggled in his early basketball career.[21] Receiving no athletic scholarship offers out of high school and being turned down by his first-choice school, Stanford University, Lin decided after six months of prayer to enroll at Harvard.

When Lin was not selected in the 2010 NBA draft after graduating from Harvard, Donnie Nelson, the president of basketball operations for the Dallas Mavericks and a committed Christian, called him and told him that God had a perfect plan for him.

Later Lin received offers to play on multiple teams, including the Mavericks, Los Angeles Lakers and Golden State Warriors. In the end, he signed with the Warriors, then was released after a year without much opportunity to play.

Eventually the New York Nicks claimed Lin off waivers but assigned him to Erie BayHawks of the D-League. After a while he was called up to fill in for injured Nicks' players, and he became an overnight sensation when he helped secure seven consecutive wins for the Nicks. He was the first NBA player to score at least 20 points and 7 assists in each of his first 4 starts.

His fame began to rise. Despite the recent fame and popularity, Lin remained committed to his game, his team and his faith. He stated,

> God's given me a unique platform and right now I am trying to use it in the right way...I can use national television, I can use the media in a way to talk about my faith, to talk about how much God has done in my life, and not what I've done to make it to the NBA.

He admits that he struggles with pride, but he constantly reminds himself that his identity lies in Christ and not his NBA career. He states,

> I'm not playing for anything on this earth, I'm playing for my prize in heaven, for the upward call that Paul talks about, that's what I need to remind myself every day when I wake up. I [have] to really understand that I'm not playing for all my fans, for my family, even for myself, I really have to play to glorify God...And when other people see me play basketball...the way I treat my teammates, the opponents, the refs, that's all a reflection of God's image and God's love so that's the stuff I try to focus on.

Every day Jeremy Lin must forget the struggles of the past and let go of the success of the present and focus on "one thing," playing for the glory of God.

Paul said, "*I press on toward the goal to win the prize*" (Philippians 3:14). It was an intentional effort on his part. He did not live in the past, he did not keep looking over his shoulder, he kept moving forward. Was he successful? At the end of his life he would clearly state,

> *The time has come for my departure. I have fought the good fight, I have finished the race, I have kept the faith. Now there is in store for me the crown of righteousness, which the Lord, the righteous Judge, will award to me on that day—and not only to me, but also to all who have longed for his appearing.* (2 Timothy 4:6–8)

As he reflected on his life Paul was able to say that he did not become discouraged and decide to quit. Despite various obstacles he ran the race and remained true and faithful to Christ, and as a result of his faithfulness he knew there was laid up for him a "*crown of righteousness*" (2 Timothy 4:8). This crown is eternal life.

This is the promise of God for all who keep looking forward with one focus in life and remain faithful to their calling as followers of Jesus Christ.

There are things in the past we need to forget. There are things in our past that are both good and bad that can overshadow the future, and we miss the eternal perspective that God intends for us. We need to be moving forward. Take some time to consider your journey of life. Are you living in the past, or do you live with an eye to the future, enjoying every moment God gives to you?

David Livingston was born into a working class family in Blantyre, Scotland, and at the age of 10 he started working at a cotton mill for 14 hours a day. At night he would study, and through Scotland's enlightened higher education system he studied medicine, first at Anderson College, Glasgow, and then at the British and Foreign Medical School in England. The year he graduated from medical school he was ordained a missionary by the London Missionary Society, and he set out for South Africa. From 1841 until his death in 1873 Livingston's aim was to bring Christianity to Africa and to end the slave trade.

During his time in Africa, Livingston returned to Britain twice, in 1856 and in 1864. In his final years it was obvious that he was beset with various health problems. While visiting Britain for what would be the last time he was asked, "Dr. Livingston, where are you ready to go now?" Livingston answered, "I am ready to go anywhere as long as it is forward." On May 1, 1873, at the age of 60, David Livingston was found dead kneeling beside his bed.

Are you looking forward?

Reflections

1. As you reflect on your life, do you have any regrets? Are these regrets negatively influencing how you live today?

_____

_____

_____

_____

2. Offer this to God and ask Him to reveal to you the certainties of your future.

_____

_____

_____

_____

3. The apostle Paul said, *"Forgetting what is behind and straining toward what is ahead, I press on toward the goal to win the prize for which God has called me heavenward in Christ Jesus"* (Philippians 3:13–14). What would that mean for you? What is the main focus of your life?

_____

_____

_____

_____

4. First Timothy 6:12–13 says, "*Fight the good fight of the faith. Take hold of the eternal life to which you were called when you made your good confession in the presence of many witnesses. In the sight of God, who gives life to everything.*" Read this slowly and listen for a word or phrase that captures your thoughts. Pray this back to God.

_____

_____

_____

Offer this prayer, based on Psalm 106:

How I praise God today!
What is so amazing to me
is the manner in which he makes hay out of straw and stubble
of my feeble efforts and foolish errors.
We rejoice when God smiles upon us,
and let it be known
how good and gracious he is.
But when we meet up with hard times
or become enslaved within the boredom of the daily routine,
we relapse into grumbling and
act as if God were far away.
How loving and patient is God!
Even when we fail him,
he never fails to love and care for us.
Even when we don't trust him
or willingly obey him,
God never ceases to pursue us
and draw us back into the circle of his love.
And he will carry out his purposes even through the failures and defeats of our life.
May he find pleasure in my life for him!
Amen.

CHAPTER FIVE
SHOW A LITTLE KINDNESS

What is desired in a man is kindness.
(Proverbs 19:22, NKJV)

Kindness is the language which the deaf can hear and the blind can see.
(African Proverb)

From time to time we hear stories of people who engage in random acts of kindness. This is an act whereby you do some good deed toward another person, perhaps someone you do not even know, without any thought of this deed being reciprocated. For example, it might be as simple as holding a door open for a stranger or stopping to help a person whose car is stuck in a snowdrift. When this occurs it is amazing how many people are actually surprised by the act of kindness, simply because they never expect it to happen.

Kindness is really an expression of tenderness or caring for another person. However, for a Christian, instead of kindness being an occasional random act, it is to be a way of life. The apostle Paul states, "*Clothe yourselves with compassion, kindness*" (Colossians 3:12). In other words, it is a lifestyle. However, this is much easier said than done, because practicing kindness is not always easy. We get busy, tired and irritable; people can annoy us, and we want to brush them off. We need to realize that kindness requires commitment, intentionality and effort.

David, the king of Israel, was a man who showed great kindness. Following the death of Saul, the first king of Israel, and Jonathan, his son, David was placed on the throne.

Living, Dying, Living Forever

For years he and Jonathan had been the closest of friends, and their love for each other was well known.

Jonathan had a son called Mephibosheth, who was crippled in both feet. As a baby he had been dropped accidently by his nurse, and this resulted in his inability to walk. Though Saul, the former king, had for many years opposed David and sought to kill him, David never retaliated. Now enthroned as king, David asked a former servant of Saul's named Ziba if there was anyone left in Saul's family to whom he could show kindness. Rather a strange request. The servant informed him that Jonathan's son Mephibosheth, who was crippled and lived in the village of Lo Debar, was the only surviving relative that he knew of. David ordered that Mephibosheth be brought into his presence.

I am sure that when Mephibosheth heard this he was somewhat unnerved. Would David seek revenge because of the actions of his grandfather?

When David met him, the first thing he said to the young man was "*Don't be afraid*" and then he added, "*I will surely show you kindness for the sake of your father Jonathan. I will restore to you all the land that belonged to your grandfather Saul, and you will always eat at my table*" (2 Samuel 9:7).

Unbelievable! David brought him into his home and treated him like his own son. What an incredible act of kindness and compassion!

Throughout the Scriptures we see the kindness of God. The Hebrew word *hesed* is translated "loving kindness," an attribute God expressed in many different ways. The Psalmist wrote, "*As a father has compassion on his children, so the LORD has compassion on those who fear him; for he knows how we are formed, he remembers that we are dust*" (Psalm 103:13–14).

In Jesus we see kindness incarnated through the interactions he had with people. One day when he was ministering he noticed that the disciples were becoming tired; in fact, they were so busy, they did not have time to grab lunch. Jesus told them to leave and get some rest, so they got into a boat and went to a solitary place. The crowds kept following Jesus around the shoreline, and when he landed on the shore, we are told, "*He had compassion on them, because they were like sheep without a shepherd*" (Mark 6:34). Showing kindness and compassion was Jesus' way of life.

So how are we to respond to all the needs around us? To answer that question, Jesus told the story that has become known as the Good Samaritan. A man was travelling along a dangerous road when he was attacked, robbed and left for dead. Along that road came three individuals, who saw the man lying in the ditch. The first two had pressing engagements, and that became their excuse for not helping the man. However the third, a man from Samaria (considered by some to be an outcast), got down and helped the man. He bandaged up his wounds and then took him to an inn, where he could recover from his beating. All this he did at his own expense. We realize that this act of kindness was an intentional commitment of time, energy and resources with no thought of repayment.

When Jesus was dying in excruciating agony, he was thinking about others. Near the cross there were several women, Mary Magdalene, Mary the wife of Clopas, his mother's sister, and of course his mother Mary, all gathered to be with him as he died. When Jesus saw his mother and the disciple whom he loved, who most assume to be John, he said to his mother, "*Dear woman, here is your son*," and to the disciple he said, "*Here is your mother*" (John 19:25–27). From that moment this disciple took Mary into his home, where she would become part of his family.

Some writers have tried to spiritualize this event, but I think it was simply the account of a son who was concerned about the well-being of his mother and was making certain she would be cared for after his death. In that culture it was the responsibility of the oldest son to take care of his mother, and since Jesus would not be able to do this anymore, he committed his mother into the care of the beloved disciple.

As followers of Jesus we are called to show kindness and compassion that is linked with the action of God for his people. The prophet Isaiah wrote,

> "*Is not this the kind of fasting I have chosen: to loose the chains of injustice and untie the cords of the yoke, to set the oppressed free and break every yoke? Is it not to share your food with the hungry and to provide the poor wanderer with shelter—when you see the naked, to clothe him, and not to turn away from your own flesh and blood?*" (Isaiah 58:6–7)

The apostle James would concur. It is not enough to claim to have faith; it must be a lived-out reality that touches the lives of people. James wrote,

> *Suppose a brother or sister is without clothes and daily food. If one of you says to him, "Go, I wish you well; keep warm and well fed," but does nothing about his physical needs, what good is it? In the same way, faith by itself, if it is not accompanied by action, is dead.* (James 2:15–17)

Our calling is to show kindness and compassion, a spiritual practice that everyone can do. Some may be thinking, "There are so many needs, and there are so few resources at my disposal; what can I do?" Begin by asking God to make you sensitive to people and to become more aware of the situations around you. St. Benedict in his Rule of Life stated that we need to receive each person as we would receive Jesus. Imagine if you made that your prayer at the beginning of each day. There are so many people we encounter. Some we consider to be a nuisance; others may take up our time; but if you saw each person as sent by God, would your attitude change? Jesus said,

> "*For I was hungry and you gave me something to eat, I was thirsty and you gave me something to drink, I was a stranger and you invited me in, I needed clothes and you clothed me, I was sick and you looked after me, I was in prison and you came to visit me... whatever you did for one of the least of these brothers of mine, you did for me.*" (Matthew 25:35–40)

Would you show kindness and compassion to Jesus?

In other situations our kindness is expressed by the comfort we offer to others. The apostle Paul wrote,

> *Praise be to the God and Father of our Lord Jesus Christ, the Father of compassion and the God of all comfort, who comforts us in all our troubles, so that we can comfort those in any trouble with the comfort we ourselves have received from God.* (2 Corinthians 1:3–4)

Paul recognized that God comforts us, but not for our sake alone. Part of the reason for God's comfort to us is that we might be able to comfort others. Only those who have received comfort are capable of comforting others.

Who are the people who need God's comfort? What are some of the compassionate practices you can do? In some instances the comfort we bring will be words of kindness or encouragement that we speak. Mother Theresa once said, "Kind words can be short and easy to speak, but their echoes are endless."

In other instances there is nothing we can say or do that will bring comfort, but we can be present. When Job lost all his possessions, his family and his health, his three friends came and simply sat with him in his grief. There were no words. Allen Verhey comments,

There were no words because there was no sense to be made of it. The structure of his world had been shattered. The meaning of his life had unravelled. His identity as a cherished child of God had been assaulted. It was the presence of his friends, silently ready to share the pain, that broke the desolating isolation of suffering and allowed Job to try to find words to express the pain and the begin to reconstruct a structure, a meaning, and an identity in the midst of it.[22]

After a period of seven days of silence, Job's friends began to speak to him about his situation. They should have remained silent, because their words were not helpful; in fact, their words threw Job into deeper despair. Verhey comments about these talkative friends,

The problem was not that they spoke, but what they said. And the problem with what they said was not that they had no answers for Job, but that they thought they had them all. They claimed to know too much and to know it too clearly. They thought they needed to be the defense attorney for God, but they ended up the as prosecutors of Job. Their words defending God and hope and humility painfully accused Job in his suffering and ironically made God out to be a nitpicker and a tyrant.[23]

Don't be worried about what you are to do; God will make that known to you on a day-to-day basis. Be sensitive to what he is showing you to do. Begin each day by committing yourself to serve God as you serve others. Perhaps it will be some in act of kindness or a word of encouragement or being present with another that you will live out the kindness and compassion of our God.

Charles Stanley tells a very touching story about a farmer who had puppies for sale. He painted a sign advertising the pups, and as he was nailing the sign to a post on the edge of his farm he noticed a little boy looking at him.

> The boy wanted to buy a puppy. The farmer told the boy that the puppies were rather expensive. The little boy reached into his pocket and produced a handful of change. All he had was thirty-nine cents. He asked if that would be enough money to at least take a look at the puppies.
>
> The farmer called the puppies and out of the doghouse came four little balls of fur. The little boy's eyes danced with delight. Then he noticed something stirring in the dog house. Slowly another little ball of fur appeared; much smaller than the rest. Down the ramp it slid, then in an awkward manner the pup began hobbling toward the others, doing its best to catch up.
>
> The little boy exclaimed, "That's the one I want."
>
> The farmer tried to discourage the little boy from buying that particular pup. He told the boy that this particular puppy would never be able to run and play with him like the other ones would.
>
> The little boy reached down and began rolling up his pant leg. In doing so he revealed a steel brace running down his leg attaching itself to a specially made shoe. Looking at the farmer the boy said, "You see, sir, I don't run too well myself, and that pup will need someone who understands."
>
> All around us there are people who need people who understand.[24]

Reflections

1. Take some time to reflect on the story of Jesus and his final words to his mother Mary and to the beloved disciples (John 19:26–27). Listen for a word or phrase that captures your attention, and then ask yourself, "How does this apply to my life?"

_____

_____

_____

_____

2. How would God have you show kindness and compassion today? Are there people whom you are aware of who need to experience a random act of kindness? What could you do?

_____

_____

_____

_____

3. How have you experienced the comfort of God? How will this enable you to bring hope into others' lives?

_____

_____

_____

_____

4. The "Theology of Presence" in essence is when we bring the presence of Christ into relationships. There will be times when we say nothing, yet our presence can bring great comfort. How have you experienced this in your life? What was it like?

_____

_____

_____

_____

5. Write a prayer asking God to enable you to be a person of kindness and compassion.

_____

_____

_____

_____

6. Read or sing this hymn.

Be Still My Soul

Be still, my soul: the Lord is on thy side.
Bear patiently the cross of grief or pain.
Leave to thy God to order and provide;
In every change, He faithful will remain.
Be still, my soul: thy best, thy heavenly Friend
Through thorny ways leads to a joyful end.
(Katharina von Schlegel)
(Public Domain)

CHAPTER SIX
A LIFE OF GRATITUDE

Give thanks in all circumstances, for this is God's will for you in Christ Jesus.
(1 Thessalonians 5:18)

To be grateful is to recognize the love of God in everything He has given us—and He has given us everything... Gratitude takes nothing for granted, is never unresponsive, is constantly awakening to new wonder and to praise of the goodness of God. For the grateful person knows

that God is good, not by hearsay but by experience. And that is what makes all the difference.
(Thomas Merton)

The spiritual practice of gratitude has been called a way of life or a state of mind. It is the awareness of all the things that have been given to us by God that leads us to expressions of gratitude. However, it is possible that we simply take a lot of things for granted.

Is gratitude a part of your life?

Gratitude does not seem to come naturally; it is something that needs to be learned. If you are a parent, you teach your children to say "Thank you," because it does not come naturally. It is something we need to do consciously, constantly and carefully.

Perhaps this is more evident today, since we live in a culture of entitlement. This is an attitude that says "life owes me something" or "people owe me something" or "God owes me something." If we do not get what we believe we are entitled to receive, we can become bitter and angry and resentful. Rabbi Dov Heller states,

> Eliminating entitlement from your life and embracing gratitude is spiritually and psychologically liberating. Gratitude is the recognition that life owes me nothing and all the good I have is a gift. Gratitude is where we begin to experience God in a powerfully personal way. "Thank you" is the simplest and most powerful prayer a person can say. If you can say, "Thank you," you can connect with God and begin to develop a personal relationship with Him.[25]

In Luke 17:11–19 there is a story about ten men who had the opportunity to express their gratitude to God, but only one of them actually said, "Thank you." Jesus was on his way to the city of Jerusalem, and as he entered a village he encountered ten men who had leprosy. They did not come close to Jesus but stood at a distance and shouted, "*Jesus, Master, have pity on us!*" The reason they did not come close to Jesus was because their disease made them ceremonially unclean, and people would become very hostile toward them if they attempted to approach anyone.

Leprosy is a disease that affects the body's nervous system, leaving pale skin patches, but as the disease progresses it can lead to numbness in the hands and feet. It is also believed leprosy can be infectious, transmitted through airborne droplets when someone sneezes or coughs.

In biblical times lepers were required to live apart from the rest of society, and to re-enter society they had to be declared clean by the priest (Leviticus 13:38–46; 14:1–32). Leprosy meant you were cut off from society, and the only people who would hang out with you were other lepers. Having the disease was a death sentence, both physically and emotionally.

In this account the ten men cry out to Jesus to be healed, and Jesus tells them to go and show themselves to the priest, who would be able to examine their skin and determine if they were healed of the disease. Normally they would not go to the priest until they had been healed, but as the New Testament scholar Darrel Bock states, "Telling them to go indicates healing will occur. If they obey Jesus they will be healed."[26]

Healed from leprosy, life would be very different for these men, as they would be able to return home and pursue a normal life. However, in this story we are told that only one man returned to Jesus to express gratitude for his healing. He was thankful that his life had been restored, and it was obvious that he did not take this healing for granted.

As Luke tells this story, there is an interesting notation. The man who expressed his gratitude was referred to as a Samaritan and a foreigner. Samaritans were disliked by the Jews because of their religious defection and intermarriage. Consequently the healing of this man was especially shocking because many would perceive him as a person beyond the realm of God's grace. In actuality what is most shocking is that the other nine who were healed (presumably Jews who understood about the mercy and kindness of God) did not return to say thanks. Did they believe they were "entitled"?

Grateful people realize God cares about them, but too often we take life for granted, and this causes our hearts to become somewhat cold. Author Ken Boa writes,

> We tend toward two extremes when we forget to remember God's ben-
> efits in our lives. The first extreme is presumption…When things are
> going "our way" we may forget God or acknowledge Him in a shallow
> or mechanical manner. The other extreme is resentment and bitterness
> due to difficult circumstances. When we suffer setbacks or losses, we
> wonder why we are not doing as well as others and develop a mindset
> of murmuring and complaining…This lack of contentment and grati-
> tude stems in part from our efforts to control the content of our lives in
> spite of what Christ may or may not desire for us to have. It also stems
> from our tendency to focus on what we do not possess rather than all
> the wonderful things we have already received.[27]

Living, Dying, Living Forever

In the Talmud there is a powerful story of a woman who understood what gratitude meant in the midst of tragic circumstances.[28] A woman named Brunia and her husband, Rabbi Meir, had two sons who both died on a Friday afternoon before Sabbath. According to Jewish law, one was not permitted to have a funeral or openly mourn on the Sabbath. Since there was nothing she could do, she decided not to tell her husband about the death of their sons until after Sabbath so he could enjoy the day.

When the Sabbath was over she knew she had to break the terrible news to her husband. So she asked him a legal question. What is the proper course of action if one person borrows two jewels from another and then the original owner requests that the jewels be returned? He replied that one is obligated to return the loan upon demand. Brunia then told her husband about the death of their two sons and said, "God has requested that we return the loan of our two jewels."

What this story is trying to tell us is that everything in life is a gift from God that is loaned to us for a period of time. Once we understand that everything is a gift we can express gratitude to God, who becomes the focus in our life rather than the things that happen.

The apostle Paul wrote, "*Give thanks in all circumstances, for this is God's will for you in Christ Jesus*" (1 Thessalonians 5:18). This does not mean that we must give thanks for literally everything that happens to us. This would be rather ludicrous. Things that happen because of the sinfulness or selfishness of us or others need to be changed, not accepted. We give thanks **in** all situations, not **for** all situations. This is an act whereby we recognize that our life is in God's hand and that we can trust in his goodness toward us. Ken Boa writes, "To give thanks is to remember the…blessings we have received and to be content with what our loving Lord provides, even when it does not correspond to what we had in mind."[29]

The apostle Paul was not an armchair theologian who casually talked about gratitude; he wrote out of the crucible of his own experiences. To the Christians in the city of Corinth he recalled many of the difficulties he experienced in life. He was shipwrecked, beaten numerous times, stoned, exposed to many dangers, knew hunger and thirst and faced daily pressure in his concerns for all the churches. Most of us can't begin to comprehend what life was like for this man. Yet in the midst of it all he chose to trust in the power of God that would enable him to cope.

Writing from a prison cell in Rome while awaiting trial and possible execution, Paul declares, "*Rejoice in the Lord always…Do not be anxious about anything, but in everything, by prayer and petition, with thanksgiving, present your requests to God*" (Philippians 4:4–6). He does not rejoice in his circumstances, but he chooses to focus on God, and in him he rejoices. Our relationship with God becomes the focus of our thanksgiving. Through all the situations Paul experienced he shares with us his unique perspective on life: "*I have learned the secret of being content in any and every situation...I can do everything through him who gives me strength*" (Philippians 4:12–13).

If we do not develop an attitude of gratitude, then ingratitude will take over our lives, and when ingratitude takes over our lives we become bitter people because we do not get what we think we deserve. It is through an attitude of gratitude that we recognize that in all aspects of life we are dependent upon God, and we can begin to see his divine intervention in our lives for our ultimate good and his glory.

For many people the annual celebration of Thanksgiving is somewhat of a perfunctory exercise in giving thanks. How can we become aware of the gifts of God on a daily basis so that thanksgiving can become a way of life? Douglas Christie tells the story about his daughter's first days in school. When she would return home after a day at school he would ask the typical question "What did you do today?" and the only response was a short list of activities. In order to have her share more of her day with him, he changed the question to "What did you notice today?"

Perhaps we need to notice what God is doing in our day, and when we do, it will lead us to express our gratitude. The Prayer of Examen developed by Ignatius of Loyola was a prayer format with one facet of the prayer focused on thanksgiving. Take a moment and think about the following questions: What am I grateful for today? Where did I feel loved, connected or energized in this day? Who are the people that touched my life this day? All of these questions help us to notice God's presence in our day and lead us to express gratitude.

Regardless of the circumstances you are facing or the stage of life you are in, today reflect on your gratitude to God and find an expression of thanksgiving.

Reflections

1. Read the story of the ten lepers in Luke 17:11–19. How do you respond to this story? What feelings seem to rise up within you? Does this tell you anything?

_____

_____

_____

_____

2. How do you express gratitude? G. K. Chesterton wrote, "You say grace before meals. All right. But I say grace before a concert, a play, before I open a book, before painting, swimming, walking, playing and before I dip the pen in ink." He found opportunities in the ordinary to give thanks. As you reflect upon the day, what do you "notice" that can lead you to thanksgiving?

_____

_____

_____

_____

3. Today, begin each activity with a prayer of thanksgiving.

4. Who are the people in your life you are grateful for? Why not give them a call, send a card or an email and simply tell them how you feel.

_____

_____

_____

_____

5. Read Psalm 100 as a prayer of gratitude.

Psalm 100

Shout for joy to the Lord, all the earth.
Worship the Lord with gladness;
come before him with joyful songs.
Know that the Lord is God.
It is he who made us, and we are his;
we are his people, the sheep of his pasture.
Enter his gates with thanksgiving
and his courts with praise;
give thanks to him and praise his name.
For the Lord is good and his love endures forever;
his faithfulness continues through all generations.

CHAPTER SEVEN
FEAR NOT!

Perfect love drives out fear.
(1 John 4:18)

The only thing we have to fear is fear itself.
(Franklin D. Roosevelt)

Everyone has experienced situations and circumstances that caused them to be afraid. Some of our fears alert us to real danger and help us avoid harm, while other fears may be irrational. We may be afraid of change, facing new situations or financial uncertainty, afraid of being alone or not knowing what the future holds.

In the Bible there are 365 admonitions to "fear not." God is aware that there are many situations and circumstances that can cause us to be afraid, and He continually says to us, "Fear not."

After Moses died God told Joshua that he was to lead the Israelites into the Promised Land. This was a challenging task, to say the least. Joshua was aware that in the previous 40 years Moses had many challenges leading the people from the captivity in Egypt to the edge of the Promised Land. As Joshua took on the leadership role, God gave him a promise: "*As I was with Moses, so I will be with you; I will never leave you nor forsake you. Be strong and courageous*" (Joshua 1:5–6). This promise by God was given to a man who could now face his fears, knowing God was with him.

One day Jesus was speaking to a large crowd of people. At the end of the day the disciples wanted to send the crowd away, but Jesus knew they were hungry and needed to

Living, Dying, Living Forever

eat. The disciples did not know what to do, since the food they had consisted of five loaves of bread and two fish, totally inadequate for so many people. Jesus instructed the people to sit down on the ground. Then he took the food, gave thanks to God, and had the disciples distribute the food among the people. When the meal was over, everyone had more than enough to eat, and there was food left over.

When supper was over Jesus had the disciples get into a boat and go to the other side of the lake while he sent the crowd home. While they were crossing the lake, a storm arose. Most of the disciples were not very good sailors, and storms on the lake could be hazardous. Jesus, knowing they could be afraid, came to them walking on the water, but this really terrified them, for they thought they had seen a ghost. At that moment Jesus spoke to them. "*Take courage! It is I. Don't be afraid*" (Matthew 14:27).

In the both accounts, Joshua taking over the leadership of the people of Israel and the disciples crossing the stormy sea in a boat, God spoke to their fear by reminding them of his presence with them. How often we forget the promise of God "I am with you." When God is with us, our fears can be conquered.

One fear many do not want to face or perhaps do not know how to face is their own death or the death of a loved one. In the back of our minds we all know that one day our deaths will occur, but we prefer to not think about it. It leaves us with an uneasy feeling. The fears associated with dying can be different for each person. Therese Rando has identified some of these fears, which may or may not be of concern to you.[30]

There is the fear of the unknown. We fear that which we do not know, or at the very least we are apprehensive. We like to feel secure. As one thinks about life and the future in the light of dying, several questions begin to emerge. What life experiences will I not be able to have? What will happen to my family and friends? What will happen to my life plans and projects? What will be my destiny in the hereafter?

There is the fear of loneliness. We like to have people around us to give us comfort, reassurance and security. When dying, many discover that they are isolated, as family and friends find it difficult to witness another's sickness and discomfort. Approximately 80 percent of people in North America die in an institutional setting, away from that which is familiar.

There is the fear of pain and suffering. We are able to endure suffering if we can make sense of it and have some hope there will be relief.

There is the fear of eternal punishment. People who are devout in their faith as well as those who do not claim any faith may fear they will be punished for what they did or did not do here on earth. There are those who say, "I tried my best" or "I hope I was a good person," but this in itself does not give the reassurance they need.

Edit

So how do we address these issues? The admonition of God is "fear not." This admonition is followed by the assurance of God's presence with us and a reminder of his character—his faithfulness, kindness or intervening power—in our time of need.

When the children of Israel were living in exile, it was uncertain what the future would be like. What would happen to them? Was there any hope for them or for their children? In this context the prophet Isaiah writes,

> "*Do not fear, for I am with you; do not be dismayed, for I am your God. I will strengthen you and help you; I will uphold you with my righteous right hand… For I am the LORD, your God, who takes hold of your right hand and says to you, Do not fear; I will help you.*" (Isaiah 41:10–13)

In other words, God is telling them, "Don't panic and look around for a way out. First and foremost look to me." This is difficult for most people to do; we are activists, and we want to be doing something to change our circumstances. God says he will do two things.

He will strengthen us. This means we need to realize that God is the one who will give us what we need in order to make it through. We cannot do some things on our own, and we need God's strength; but to receive that strength we must wait upon God. Isaiah wrote,

> *The LORD is the everlasting God, the Creator of the ends of the earth. He will not grow tired or weary…He gives strength to the weary and increases the power of the weak…those who hope in the LORD will renew their strength. They will soar on wings like eagles; they will run and not grow weary, they will walk and not be faint.* (Isaiah 40:28–31)

He will uphold us with his righteous right hand. The right hand of God is a metaphor to express the power and presence of God. But it is also his righteous right hand. The righteousness of God refers to his character, his grace and his unconditional love. So we can be assured that we will be kept safe in the powerful loving care of Almighty God.

Those who fear loneliness can be assured of God's abiding presence. When my mother was dying, she seemed to be afraid. When I asked her if she was afraid to die, she replied, "No, it is not dying that I fear; it is leaving all those I love." I suppose this could be described clinically as "separation anxiety," the fear we experience when we are separated from those whom we love. However, a clinical understanding of separation anxiety is not helpful for those who are dying! We need the assurance of the One who will be with us through death and beyond. The Psalmist wrote, "*Even though I walk through the valley of the shadow of death, I will fear no evil, for you are with me*" (Psalm 23:4). This is the assurance of God's abiding presence in life and in death.

Those who fear suffering and pain can identify with the apostle Paul, who three times asked God to remove what he referred to as "*a thorn in my flesh*" (2 Corinthians 12:7). God chose not to do so but told Paul, "*My grace is sufficient for you, for my power is made perfect in weakness*" (2 Corinthians 12:9). The promise of God is that he will enable you and strengthen you, no matter what you are going through, if you will ask him to do so. God's grace will be more than sufficient at the time of our need.

Those who fear eternal punishment need to be assured of the mercy and grace of God. The apostle Paul declared that once he was a blasphemer, a persecutor and a violent man; in fact, he described himself as the worst of sinners. But regardless of his past, he was shown mercy through the grace of the Lord Jesus that was poured out on him (1 Timothy 1:13ff). As we turn our hearts toward God and seek his forgiveness for our sins, the promise is that they are forgiven and that God remembers them no more. Our sins are forgiven because Jesus paid the penalty that we deserve. He died in our place. Paul would write, "*Therefore, there is now no condemnation for those who are in Christ Jesus, because through Christ Jesus the law of the Spirit of life set me free from the law of sin and death*" (Romans 8:1–2). Since there is no condemnation, there is neither judgment nor punishment.

We need to understand that God is for us. He will not leave us alone and helpless; therefore we need not fear. Focus on him and not on your fears. Claim his promises. Read these words of the Psalmist and let them speak to the fears you have:

> *I sought the Lord, and he answered me; he delivered me from all my fears. Those who look to him are radiant; their faces are never covered with shame. This poor man called, and the Lord heard him; he saved him out of all his troubles. The angel of the Lord encamps around those who fear him, and he delivers them. Taste and see that the Lord is good; blessed is the man who takes refuge in him.* (Psalm 34:4–8)

Reflection

1. Lloyd Ogilvie, a pastor and author, suggests four basic steps to deal with fear.[31]

a. Step One: Describe your fears. Many people live with a generalized list, but we need to single them out one by one if we are going to deal with them. What causes you to be afraid? Take some time and ask God to help you understand the fears you have. Write out what you fear.

Fear of the unknown
Fear of the loss of loved ones
Fear of pain and suffering
Fear of eternal punishment
Other _____

b. Step Two: Dissect the fear. Is the fear based in an actual person or situation, or is it an irrational fear? We can only deal with reality. So ask yourself this question: "What am I really afraid of?" This will enable you to get to the core issue.

c. Step Three: Disown the fear. To do this we need to surrender the fear to God. Some people hang on to their fears, and it becomes a way of life. So you have a choice: keep the fear, or give it to God. We need to realize that there is nothing too difficult for God to handle, and that includes our fears.

d. Step Four: Displace the fear. The apostle John, who was with the other disciples in the boat on that night when they were so afraid, later wrote, "*There is no fear in love. But perfect love drives out fear, because fear has to do with punishment. The one who fears is not made perfect in love*" (1 John 4:18). Our fears can be replaced when we realize that we are loved by God, who is always with us. So when I am afraid I choose to focus on the relationship I have with him and not on my fears. I am loved by him, and his love is stronger than my fear.

2. Read the following texts that address the topic of fear and see how you can apply them to your life.

a. "*Even though I walk through the valley of the shadow of death, I will fear no evil, for you are with me*" (Psalm 23:4).

b. "*Do not be anxious about anything, but in everything by prayer and supplication with thanksgiving let your requests be made known to God. And the peace of God, which surpasses all understanding, will guard your hearts and your minds in Christ Jesus*" (Philippians 4:6–7, ESV).

c. "*Humble yourselves, therefore, under the mighty hand of God so that at the proper time he may exalt you, casting all your anxieties on him, because he cares for you*" (1 Peter 5:6–7, ESV).

d. "*Fear not, for I am with you; be not dismayed, for I am your God; I will you strengthen you, I will help you, I will uphold you with my righteous right hand*" (Isaiah 41:10, ESV).

Living, Dying, Living Forever

_____

_____

_____

_____

_____

_____

_____

_____

_____

_____

_____

_____

_____

_____

_____

_____

_____

_____

_____

_____

_____

_____

_____

_____

_____

_____

_____

_____

_____

_____

_____

_____

_____

_____

_____

Write out your response:

_____

_____

_____

_____

3. The following are a series of breath prayers. They are intended to be repeated slowly until the truth of the prayer moves from your head to your heart. Choose one of these short prayers and offer it up to God this day. Perhaps you will choose another one tomorrow.

a. "_Be still, and know that I am God_" (Psalm 46:10).

b. "_The LORD is my shepherd, I shall not be in want_" (Psalm 23:1).

c. "_Even though I walk through the valley of the shadow of death, I will fear no evil_" (Psalm 23:4).

d. "_My peace I give you_" (John 14:27).

e. "_Cast all your anxiety on him because he cares for you_" (1 Peter 5:7).

f. "_I am with you always, to the very end of the age_" (Matthew 28:20).

g. "_I have loved you with an everlasting love_" (Jeremiah 31:3).

CHAPTER EIGHT
AHH, PEACE

Now may the Lord of peace himself give you peace at all times and in every way.
(2 Thessalonians 3:16)

God cannot give us happiness and peace apart from Himself because it is not there. There is no such thing.
(C. S. Lewis)[32]

It was said of the late Elvis Presley that he would have paid one million dollars for a week of peace of mind. The reality is that everyone is under stress, and as the stress builds we become anxious and upset. Quite possibly you can identify some element of stress in your life even at this present moment. Some try to cope with stress by taking medication or consuming alcohol or exercising or by reading self-help books. Interestingly, God has an antidote to stress, which is peace. But what is this peace that God offers?

There are two types of peace we want to consider. First we must have peace with God. The apostle Paul writing to the Christians in Rome said, "*Since we have been justified through faith, we have peace with God through our Lord Jesus Christ*" (Romans 5:1). We cannot have peace until we know God. The reformer Martin Luther sought to have this inner peace with God by performing good deeds and carrying out religious activities, all to no avail. Only when he placed his faith in Jesus Christ and not in all his external religious activities did he discover the peace that God offered.

In the Bible one of the names of God is Jehovah-Shalom, which means "Jehovah my Peace." God created humankind to have a relationship with him whereby they would know they are loved and cared for and thus experience his presence and peace in all of life. He would be to us Jehovah-Shalom. Yet the sad reality is that many do not have the relationship God intended and consequently do not experience the peace God gives.

The author Lloyd Ogilvie writes,

> Knowing God begins with the astounding assurance that, in spite of what we've done or been, his love for us will never change. We were created by God to be loved by him and for us to love him. We experience an intimate union with God when we receive his love, accept his forgiveness, and turn our lives over to his control. We know who we are when we accept whose we are. This is the secure source of peace.[33]

If the first aspect of peace is peace "with" God, the second aspect of peace is the peace "of" God. Colossians 3:15 states, "*Let the peace of Christ rule in your hearts.*" There are many things in life that can cause us to be upset and rob us of peace. Here Paul tells us to let the peace of Christ rule in our hearts. The meaning of the verb "rule" comes from an athletic term, and the verse could be translated "Let the peace of Christ be the umpire in your heart." The role of an umpire in a game is to make sure that a game is played correctly by making decisions on matters of dispute or priority. If there is a disagreement between players, the umpire is the one to sort things out.

We all have situations and people in our lives that can cause upheaval, upset or conflict. There can be feelings of love, hatred, fear, distrust or concern. How do we handle all of this? The text tells us that Christ is to be the umpire of all that can cause conflict or stress in our interpersonal relationships. He is the one we turn to help us sort out the issues; we ask him to rule on our behaviours and whatever distresses us about others. This includes those in our family, our community and our church. The apostle Paul connects this with his instructions in Romans 12:18: "*If it possible, as far as it depends on you, live at peace with everyone.*" We desperately need this in our relationships. As I experience peace with Christ, I need to surrender to him all those situations and people that could rob me of my peace and ask him to enable me to find ways to live peaceably with everyone.

At the same time we need to realize that God does not always resolve issues immediately or transform our situation. But he does do some amazing things.

The Psalmist wrote, "*God is our refuge and strength, an ever-present help in trouble*" (Psalm 46:1). This psalm was written during the time of Hezekiah when the nation of Israel was under attack from the Assyrians. The enemy soldiers surrounded the city of Jerusalem, and the inhabitants were extremely anxious. To their great surprise the Assyrians were struck by a plague, and the city and the inhabitants were saved from disaster. This psalm is a reminder that regardless of the situation we may find ourselves in, God is with us, and no matter the odds against us, God is there to help us.

Jesus promised to his disciples that he would give them peace, but he also told them that because they were his followers they would experience trouble in this world. Some would be persecuted, some would be rejected by their families and others would be misunderstood. Even though these things would happen, Jesus promised he would never leave them. It would be his presence with them that would be the source of their peace. The peace of God is that reality that comes from a relationship with God.

When situations are stressful we find ourselves wanting to be active; we want to do something to bring about change so that our life is brought back into a state of equilibrium. The Psalmist has very clear instructions as to what we are to do: "*Be still, and know that I am God*" (Psalm 46:10). Being still is really an act of trusting God, and in the stillness we need to focus on God and the relationship we have with him. If he is our refuge, then we will find shelter in him. If he is our strength, then we will not be overcome by whatever situation we face.

We need to recognize that our part in all of this is to trust God. The writer of Proverbs states, "*Trust in the LORD with all your heart and lean not on your own understanding; in all your ways acknowledge him, and he will make your paths straight*" (Proverbs 3:5–6).

There are numerous examples of people who have lived out these principles. In the early church King Herod arrested and persecuted some who were followers of Jesus. James the Apostle was executed, and Peter was put into prison. Herod wanted to bring Peter to trial, with the intent of putting him to death as he had James. While in prison Peter was chained between two soldiers, and two additional sentries were posted outside his prison cell. That night in the prison cell Peter was sound asleep. In fact we are told that the angel of the Lord appeared and had to strike Peter on his side to wake him up. Immediately his chains fell off and he was led out of the prison by the angel. They passed the first and second guard and came to the city gate, which opened by itself, and they went through. They walked together the length of one street, and then the angel left him (Acts 12:1–10). Apart from God's miraculous intervention, it is intriguing that Peter was sound asleep in his prison cell. How could that be? Most of us in a similar circumstance would be so anxious, wondering what was going to happen in the morning, that we would pass the night pacing the cell floor. Peter was able to sleep because he trusted his life into the hands of God.

When we trust in the Lord with all our heart (Proverbs 3:5), we discover the peace of God. Recognizing that our life belongs to him, that he is sovereign over all circumstances and that he never makes mistakes, our trust and confidence grows. Author Rick Warren stated,

> God never has to say, "Oops!" because he never makes a mistake. Everything that happens in your life fits into God's plan for you. He uses every situation- even the problems and heartaches and difficulties you bring on yourself- to work out his purpose in your life. He fits everything perfectly into his plan for you. All God expects from you is that you trust him without trying to figure everything out. Acknowledge that God is in control.[34]

What is robbing you of peace? You may be grieving the death of a loved one or the loss of a relationship that has devastated you. You may have lost your job or your life savings. You may have come down with a serious illness or received news that you have a terminal illness. At this moment you need to know the peace of God.

Toward the end of his life while waiting in a prison cell Paul wrote, "*Do not be anxious about anything, but in everything, by prayer and petition, with thanksgiving, present your requests to God. And the peace of God, which transcends all understanding, will guard your hearts and your minds in Christ Jesus*" (Philippians 4:6–7). Instead of becoming stressed out and anxious, we are to come to God in prayer. Instead of giving our attention to that which worries us, we need to give our attention to God, asking him to give us peace in the midst of all that upsets us. As we pray, we give thanks. This does not mean we are grateful for what is stressing us out, since that is not realistic. We give thanks to God for providing what he knows is best for us in the situation. Paul spoke of this in his letter to the Thessalonians. "*In everything give thanks; for this is the will of God in Christ Jesus for you*" (1 Thessalonians 5:18, NKJV). When we pray this way we are relinquishing our control over the situation and at the same time committing ourselves into the care of Almighty God.

When we do this we discover the peace of God, which will guard our hearts and minds. In other words, God's peace is like a soldier posted on the wall, watching over us and defending us from thoughts and emotions that could upset our peace.

As you become anxious, stressed and upset, remind yourself that God is with you, that you are loved by him and that he has only your best interests in his heart. In all things keep your focus on God and not on the situation, and you will find peace. Isaiah the

Prophet declared, *"You will keep in perfect peace him whose mind is steadfast, because he trusts in you. Trust in the LORD forever, for the LORD, the LORD, is the Rock eternal"* (Isaiah 26:3–4). (2)

Reflections

1. Read the story of Peter in prison and his release by the angel of the Lord (Acts 12:1–10).
How does this account enable you to trust God to give you peace in your life?

_____

_____

_____

_____

2. Take some time to reflect upon what is robbing you of peace. Now write it out.

_____

_____

_____

_____

3. Read these words: *"Do not be anxious about anything, but in everything, by prayer and petition, with thanksgiving, present your requests to God."*
Write out your request.

_____

_____

_____

_____

Prayers of petition remind us of our dependency upon God. Jesus urged his disciples to *"Ask and it will be given to you; seek and you will find; knock and the door will be opened to you. For everyone who asks receives; he who seeks finds; and to him who knocks, the door will be opened"* (Matthew 7:7–8).

4. Pray these prayers:

> Give us within our own hearts the peace that passes understanding.
> Take from us the worries which distract us, and give us more trust.
> Take from us the doubts which disturb us, and make us
> More sure of what we believe.
> Take from us the wrong desires from which our temptation come,
> And make us more pure in heart.

Take from us the false ambitions which drive us,
And make us more content to serve you where we are and as we are.
Take from us all the estrangement from you and give us the peace of sins forgiven.
All this we ask through Jesus Christ our Lord.
Amen.
(William Barclay)[35]

The peace of God, which passes all understanding, keep our hearts and minds in the knowledge and love of God, and of his Son Jesus Christ our Lord, and may the blessings of God Almighty, the Father, the Son and the Holy Spirit, be among us and remain with us always.
Amen.[36]

5. Read this blessing.

May God give you…
For every storm a rainbow,
For every tear a smile
For every care a promise and a blessing in each trial.
For every problem life sends,
A faithful friend to share,
For every sigh a sweet song and an answer for each prayer.
(Irish Blessing)

CHAPTER NINE

LIVING WITH UNCERTAINTIES

"I do believe; help me overcome my unbelief!"
(Mark 9:24)

Believe your beliefs and doubt your doubts.
(F. F. Bosworth)

Doubt is an experience common to everyone. Is it possible to believe in God and all of his promises yet have doubts that trouble us? Some people are hindered by their doubts, while others see them as an opportunity to discover more about God and their relationship with him.

A few years ago on an adventure holiday I tried zip-lining. Actually, I am not very comfortable with heights. I love to fly in airplanes, but to look over the ledge of a high building is another matter. I went to the zip line centre and at the staging area was given instructions. A harness was strapped on me, and suddenly I found myself at the edge of a platform hundreds of feet above the earth. I had to make a choice. Would I go back to the parking lot, or would I trust myself to the process? The term "leap of faith" came to mind. A leap of faith is not about acting on something you do not believe to be true, but it is a commitment to action in spite of one's doubts. So I jumped!

There are many people in the Bible who had doubts. Childless Abraham was told by God that his offspring would be as numerous as the stars in the night sky. Years passed, yet there was no child for him and his wife, Sarah, to nurture and care for. When Abram was

99, God visited him and told him he would be the "*father of many nations*" (Genesis 17:5), and God changed his name from Abram to Abraham to signify the promise. God also told Abraham that he would bless Sarah and she would become the mother of nations. When Abraham heard this he laughed and said to himself, "*Will a son be born to a man a hundred years old? Will Sarah bear a child at the age of ninety?*" (Genesis 17:17). Abraham had serious doubts about the promise of God.

One day a man approached Jesus and pleaded with him to restore his son to health. The child was ill and had seizures that caused him to fall into open fires or pools of water. Imagine the scars this child had on his body. Imagine what it would be like to be the father, not knowing if your child might be injured or fall at anytime into a pool of water and drown.

The father had taken his son to the disciples of Jesus to see if they could heal him, but it was to no avail. When the boy was brought to Jesus he immediately began to convulse and fell to the ground, foaming at the mouth. The father cried out to Jesus, "*If you can do anything, take pity on us and help us.*" The response of Jesus is very revealing. "*'If I can?' said Jesus. 'Everything is possible for him who believes.' Immediately the boy's father exclaimed, 'I do believe; help me overcome my unbelief!'*" (Mark 9:22–24). He wanted to believe, but he had his doubts.

In the Gospel of John we discover that Jesus had three special friends, Mary, Martha and Lazarus, who lived in the village of Bethany (John 11:1–37). Lazarus became ill, and the sisters sent word to Jesus that he was ill and they wanted Jesus to come and restore him to health. However, Jesus delayed his departure, and by the time he arrived in Bethany, Lazarus had died and had been buried for four days. The first sister to greet Jesus when he arrived was Martha. She said to him, "*Lord…if you had been here, my brother would not have died.*" Then she said something even more startling.

> "*But I know that even now God will give you whatever you ask.*" Jesus said to her, "*Your brother will rise again.*" Martha answered, "*I know he will rise again in the resurrection at the last day.*" Jesus said to her, "*I am the resurrection and the life. He who believes in me will live, even though he dies; and whoever lives and believes in me will never die. Do you believe this?*" (John 11:22–26).

Martha had doubts! Martha believed that Jesus was the Messiah but had serious doubts about his power over life and death.

In your spiritual journey you may find yourself among those who have doubts. On the other hand, there are some who never seem to have any doubts; they simply believe. There are bumper sticker that declare, "God said it; I believe it, that settles it." Such statements leave no room for questions or doubt of any kind. The author Phillip Yancey contends that inquisitiveness and questioning are inevitable parts of faith. Where there is certainty, there is no room for faith. But we must learn to doubt our doubts as much as we doubt our faith.[37]

What are we doing with our doubts and the questions that are not resolved? Is the Christian faith simply holding to specific beliefs? No! William Barclay once said that faith is not an intellectual acceptance of a body of doctrine; faith is faith in a person. When you consider your relationships you realize you cannot develop a relationship apart from trust. The pastor and author John Ortberg in his book *Faith and Doubt* states, "Trust is something that happens between people. It is what holds the world of personal relationships together."[38]

Have you ever noticed that children are very trusting but that trust seems to diminish as one grows into adolescence and adulthood? Philosopher Kerry Walters has an interesting insight into this. He writes,

> Everyone is familiar with the experience in which participants are supposed to fall backwards into the waiting arms of another person. Children have no problem with this, especially if the person assigned to catch them is a grown up. But adults are notoriously bad at letting themselves go, even when the person waiting to catch them is a spouse or a close friend. The thought of placing our fate in the hands of others chills us because we distrust their willingness or ability to protect us.[39]

The reason for this, contends Walters, is that trust implies dependency, and as we become older we want to be in control.

The writer to the Hebrews states, "*Without faith it is impossible to please God*" (Hebrews 11:6). As we think about life and wrestle with doubts, we must focus on the one in whom our faith rests; it is all about our relationship with God. We need to ask these questions: Is God trustworthy? Is God faithful to his promises? Does God care about our well-being? Is there evidence that God is still the unchanging one who will always be with us, even though our feelings may vacillate and we do not sense his presence?

When life takes us through the unexpected and we begin to feel overwhelmed, doubts may surface. At times like this, when we have doubts, we can discover that it is an opportunity to grow in our faith by trusting God more and more.

We return to the three stories.

Living, Dying, Living Forever

After God made the promise to Abraham, three visitors came and informed him that within the next year he and Sarah would have a child. When the child was born Sarah exclaimed, "*Who would have said to Abraham that Sarah would nurse children? Yet I have borne him a son in his old age*" (Genesis 21:7). Abraham and Sarah had their doubts, but the visitor who told them of the promise God had made—a promise that seemed impossible—asked Abraham one question: "*Is anything too hard for the Lord?*" (Genesis 18:14). In the face of our doubts this is an important question for each one of us to consider. The writer to the Hebrews states, "*By faith Abraham, even though he was past age—and Sarah herself was barren—was enabled to become a father because he considered him faithful who had made the promise*" (Hebrews 11:11).

The man with the little boy who was sick had doubts. The disciples struggled with their faith. They had been commissioned by Jesus to "*heal the sick, raise the dead, cleanse lepers, cast out demons*" (Matthew 10:8, ESV), yet in this instance they were not able to help this child. When they inquired why they could not heal the child, Jesus revealed to them it was "*Because of your little faith*" (Matthew 17:20, ESV). It is easy to claim to have faith when life is going well and there are no challenges, but great faith develops when we choose to trust God even when we do not understand everything and face challenging situations. Over time the disciples would learn many lessons about faith and doubt, and it was through these experiences that their relationship with God matured.

When Jesus showed up four days after Lazarus died, Martha was distressed, but she along with others made their way to the tomb where Lazarus was buried. When Jesus wanted to have the grave of Lazarus opened, Martha was horrified, because her brother had been dead for four days and there would be a bad odour. Lazarus was dead; what could Jesus possibly do? Aware of her doubts, Jesus spoke directly to her and said, "*Did I not tell you that if you believed, you would see the glory of God?*" (John 11:40). Then Jesus called Lazarus to come out of the tomb, and the man who had been dead four days emerged, wrapped in linen cloths. Everyone present saw the power of God over death, and many who came to grieve with the family saw what Jesus did and put their faith in him.

I read these stories, and my faith is strengthened. There are times when I have doubts. I have never seen a dead person come back to life, so what assurance do I have that Jesus has the power over death? I read the account of Jesus raising Lazarus from the dead, and I believe it is true. I read the account Jesus' resurrection from the dead, and the evidence points to the veracity of the events, and I believe them to be true. But most importantly, I believe because I trust in Jesus. This relationship I have with him is one built on trust, and I am learning to trust him more and more day by day. The theologian William Sloan Coffin once stated, "Faith isn't believing without proof—it is trusting without reservation." As I learn to trust God in all circumstances, even with my doubts, it becomes an opportunity for my relationship with him to grow.

Reflection

1. Recognize that doubt is part of your relationship with God. What are some of the doubts you face?

_____

_____

_____

_____

2. Examine your doubts. Ask God to give you insight into the questions you face. Explore what the Bible has to say about some of these questions. Question your doubts as much as you question your beliefs.

_____

_____

_____

_____

3. Take some time to meditate on one of the belief statements of the Christian faith. Take it phrase by phrase and ask yourself, "Do I believe this? Why?" If you have doubts ask yourself, "Why?"

> I believe in God the Father almighty, creator of heaven and earth.
> I believe in Jesus Christ, his only Son, our Lord.
> He was conceived by the power of the Holy Spirit and born of the virgin Mary.
> He suffered under Pontius Pilate, was crucified, died and was buried.
> He descended to the dead.
> On the third day he rose again.
> He ascended into heaven, and is seated at the right hand of the Father.
> He will come again to judge the living and the dead.
> I believe in the Holy Spirit,
> the holy catholic church,
> the communion of saints,
> the forgiveness of sins,
> the resurrection of the body,
> and the life everlasting.
> Amen.

_____

_____

_____

4. Jesus said, "*I am the resurrection and the life. He who believes in me will live even though he dies, and whoever lives and believes in me will never die*" (John 11:25–26). Do you have any doubts about this? If you do, write them out and give it to God as a prayer.

_____

_____

_____

_____

5. Offer the following prayer.

> We Would Know More of You
> You are the God of all truth, the God of deep hiddenness.
> God of all hiddenness who shows yourself in your being hidden,
> who hides yourself in your disclosures,
> we would know more of you
> of your goodness and mercy,
> of your large purposes and long-term dreams.
> In your presence we become aware of how little we know of ourselves,
> of our interests and passions,
> of our fears and doubts,
> of our own wonderments and gifts.
> In your truthfulness, let us know more of you
> and in knowing you, ourselves as well.
> We pray in the name of Jesus, where we see you fully,
> and ourselves clearly.
> Amen.[40]

6. Memorize: "*Be merciful to those who doubt*" (Jude 1:22).

CHAPTER TEN
WHEN YOU SUFFER

We also rejoice in our sufferings, because we know that suffering produces perseverance; perseverance, character; and character, hope. And hope does not disappoint us, because God has poured out his love into our hearts by the Holy Spirit.
(Romans 5:3–5)

People are like stained glass windows. They sparkle and shine when the sun is out, but when the darkness sets in, their true

beauty is revealed only if there is light from within.
(Elisabeth Kubler Ross)

Suffering is a part of life no one can avoid, and it can take various forms of expression, whether it is physical, emotional, relational or spiritual. When Jesus called people to come and follow him, he made it clear it would involve suffering. He stated, "*If anyone would come after me, he must deny himself and take up his cross daily and follow me. For whoever wants to save his life will lose it, but whoever loses his life for me will save it*" (Luke 9:23–24).

When we reflect upon Jesus' life we know that he experienced many different forms of suffering, and at the end he died an agonizing death. The followers of Jesus should not be surprised if they too experience suffering for the sake of Christ. The apostle Peter wrote,

> *Since Christ suffered in his body, arm yourselves also with the same attitude, because he who has suffered in his body is done with sin. As a result, he does not live the rest of his earthly life for evil human desires, but rather for the will of God…So then, those who suffer according to God's will should commit themselves to their faithful Creator and continue to do good* (1 Peter 4:1–9).

During the early years of the Church many experienced severe persecution by a succession of Roman emperors. Most of the apostles suffered martyrdom in one form or another. In recent years, and even at the present moment, thousands of Christians have been tortured and imprisoned for their faith in Christ. We should not be surprised, because Jesus warned that this would happen.

There is suffering that causes a great deal of emotional pain. We can feel the sadness in Paul's voice as he wrote about those whom he loved who had deserted him and hurt him deeply. "*Demas, because he loved this world, has deserted me…Alexander the metalworker did me a great deal of harm*" (2 Timothy 4:10, 14). In his writings, we see the pain he experienced when people did not believe the message that Jesus was the Messiah. "*I have great sorrow and unceasing anguish in my heart. For I could wish that I myself were cursed and cut off from Christ for the sake of my brothers*" (Romans 9:2–3).

Suffering is difficult to fully comprehend. Theologian Abigail Evans writes,

Suffering is anguish, a threat to who we are, to our composure, to our identity. Sometimes it is a spiritual response to a physical pain. Suffering may be subtle and slow, like growing old…Suffering may be from a feeling of emptiness that results from the loss of loved ones…But the fear of death permeates all experiences of suffering, which at its heart reflects humanity's vulnerability and creatureliness.[41]

As we look at Scripture we discover several sources for suffering. First, we need to recognize that we live in a fallen world, and sin and suffering are a reality we can't escape. Second, some suffering is the result of the choices we have made. In spite of this, the Bible makes it clear that God can take our suffering and use it in a redemptive manner if we are open to learn from him.

In the Old Testament we have the classic story of Job. He seemed to have everything, and eventually everything was taken from him except his life. He lost his possessions, his children, his friends and eventually his health. Job was encouraged by his wife to "*Curse God and die!*" (Job 2:9).

Job struggled because he simply did not know why these terrible things were happening to him, and when we suffer without understanding the meaning or purpose of it all, it can lead to despair. Things got so bad for Job that he actually cursed the day he was born. He stated, "*Why did I not die at birth? Why did I not perish when I came from the womb? Why did the knees receive me? Or why the breasts, that I should nurse? For now I would have lain still and been quiet, I would have been asleep; Then I would have been at rest*" (Job 3:11–13, NKJV).

Job did not understand the purpose of his suffering, and consequently despair became his companion. There are many who when they suffer address the issue in a very straightforward manner. Why? Why me? Why now?

However, if we understand the purpose of the suffering and pain, it give us a totally different perspective. The theologian R. C. Sproul illuminates this concept by contrasting the pain and suffering in childbirth with the pain and suffering of those who have a terminal illness. He writes,

A woman who endures the travail of childbirth is able to do so because she knows that the end result will be a new life. Those who are terminally ill do not have the same hope of a good result as in childbearing. Here the pain appears to be unto death rather than unto life. Indeed that would be true if there is no salvation. If death is the end then suffering that attends to it would drive us to despair. The message of Christ is that death is not unto death but unto life.[42]

Initially Job did not grasp the reason or purpose behind his suffering, and we see him yelling at God. He did not understand what was happening or why it was happening to him. It did not make sense. But Job teaches us through his experience that we can be honest with God about our situation, even if it means we are angry with God. Abigail Evans, quoting David Watson, a British Anglican evangelist who died from cancer, stated,

> When we feel angry, bitter, helpless, or in despair, we need to be honest with God about our feelings. "In fact, it is much better expressing our anguish to God than talking resentfully about God to others. God can take on anger. Indeed he did take our anger and all our other sins when his Son died on a cross for us. He wants us to be honest with him and not to put on a pious mask when we approach him."[43]

I am sure everyone would rather not have to experience suffering, but this is not going to happen. Therefore we need to consider how we will respond. In fact, the way we respond may be a key to our endurance, and it can be an opportunity for spiritual growth and development.

The apostle Paul was not a stranger to suffering, and the various accounts of his experiences in the New Testament give us some insight to the manner in which he responded to suffering. Although he suffered in a variety of ways, there is one account in his letter to the church at Corinth that refers to his "*thorn in my flesh*" (2 Corinthians 12:7). Many people have tried to figure this out. Was it malaria or an eye disease? Some would suggest that the thorn in the flesh was not a physical ailment but rather a reference to people who opposed his ministry and caused him great harm. This is quite possible, since the term "thorn in the flesh" as used in the Old Testament was a reference to the enemies of Israel (Numbers 33:55; Joshua 23:13). Whether his suffering was the result of a physical ailment or a problematic relationship, we can identify with his pain, even if the exact nature of his problem is not known.

In this particular incident Paul pleaded with the Lord three times to take away his suffering. After the third petition the Lord told Paul not to ask again for this thorn to be removed. It was not going to happen. Paul would discover God's sufficiency to meet his deepest needs, and God would supply him with his grace at the time of need. There are times when our suffering will draw us close to God, and there we discover that he alone can meet the deepest need of the human heart.

Although we realize that suffering and death are part of the reality of life, it is essential to understand that life here on earth is not all there is, nor is it the end of the story. God has something far better for us. The apostle Paul wrote, "*I consider that our present sufferings are not worth comparing with the glory that will be revealed in us*" (Romans 8:18). If life is a journey, we need to consider what is ahead of us. Heaven is the end goal of the journey. The theologian Alistair McGrath writes, "We need to think more about the hope of eternal life, of the resurrection of our frail and mortal bodies in the likeness of Christ's glorious resurrection body, and the ultimate prize of standing, redeemed in the presence of God."[44]

However, he acknowledges, "However we choose to describe it, the promise and hope of our transfiguration of suffering are an integral part of the Christian faith."[45] In fact, he writes, "This glorious thread is woven so deeply into the fabric of our faith that it cannot possibly be removed."[46]

We will not be exempt from pain and suffering, but as we look at the big picture we begin to see there is so much more than just the here and now. There is a life to come where we will share in the glory of God. So we always live with hope.

At times, however, we need to share our suffering with others. In our Western culture this is somewhat difficult, simply because we tend to be very private and reluctant to share what is happening to us, since it might be perceived as weakness. Or perhaps we believe others are not really interested in our situation, either because they can't do anything about it or because with their busy lifestyles they simply do not have the time to spend with us.

The Christian community is not about isolation but about life together. Our life in Christ is not meant to be solitary but one that is shared with one another. If we live in isolation, it only intensifies the pain, but when we share our struggles with each other, it is a great help. The apostle Paul wrote that as community we can offer to one another support though acts of compassion and comfort. "*Praise be to the God and Father of our Lord Jesus Christ, the Father of compassion and the God of all comfort, who comforts us in all our troubles, so that we can comfort those in any trouble with the comfort we ourselves have received from God*" (2 Corinthians 1:3–4).

Jesus was well known for his acts of compassion. He healed the sick, the blind and the lame. He was a friend to the outcast and the stranger. He always had time for people. As we have experienced the compassion of God, we are called to be compassionate toward others. The author Tonya Armstrong writes,

> Close examination of the quality of compassion we have received from God will result in the quality of compassion and comfort that we express to the body of Christ, as well as to those "in any trouble." Rather than becoming bankrupt in the character of our service, we discover a rich reservoir out of which flows the infinite compassion of God, by God's people, for God's people. However, this fluid process is not automatic; on the contrary it requires intentionality, commitment, and the disciplined life.[47]

Living, Dying, Living Forever

Abigail Evans sees community as a place of transparency:

> Amazingly enough, in joining in solidarity with other's suffering, we can gain strength. Too often it has been assumed that the person of faith lives in a kind of perpetual smile, a constant upbeat frame of mind. This is not true of course, and nothing either in the New Testament or in Christian experience could justify such an attitude. The Christian rejoices with those who rejoice and weeps with those who weep (Rm. 12:15). We are called not simply to notice those who suffer and to sympathize with them, but also to identify with their pain and in the deceptions about power in which they are entangled. In short Christians have no secure and happy vantage point from which to view sorrow and pain. We are to share in the sufferings of others.[48]

Our life in Christ is not a solitary life but one that is shared with others. The writer of Ecclesiastes states,

> Two are better than one, because they have a good return for their work: If one falls down, his friend can help him up. But pity the man who falls and has no one to help him up! Also, if two lie down together, they will keep warm. But how can one keep warm alone? Though one may be overpowered, two can defend themselves. A cord of three strands is not quickly broken (Ecclesiastes 4:9–12)

So, who is there for you? Who are you available to help and comfort in their struggles and suffering?

Reflections

1. Suffering can have many different faces, physical, emotional, relational, spiritual. How would you describe what you are experiencing?

_____
_____
_____
_____

2. Do you have moments of despair? What are they? Read 2 Corinthians 4:8–18. How do you identify with this experience of Paul? How can verses 17–18 help you?

_____
_____
_____
_____

3. Sharing your suffering with others seems to be an important biblical principle (2 Corinthians 1:3–7). Are you able to do this? With whom? Do you find yourself resisting this idea? Take some time to write out what you would like to share about your present experience.

_____

_____

_____

_____

4. Are you able to discover any purpose in your suffering? How is it changing you?

_____

_____

_____

_____

5. Reflect on the words of this hymn. Let it speak as a prayer to your soul, and rest in the assurance of God's eternal presence.

Abide with Me

Abide with me, fast falls the eventide;
The darkness deepens; Lord, with me abide.
When other helpers fail and comforts flee,
Help of the helpless, O abide with me.

I need your presence every passing hour.
What but your power can foil the tempter's power?
Who like thyself my guide and strength can be?
Through cloud and sunshine, Lord, abide with me.

Hold now thy cross before my closing eyes;
Shine through the gloom and point me to the skies!
Heaven's morning breaks, and earth's vain shadows flee:
In life, in death, O Lord, abide with me!

Henry Francis Lyte
(public domain)

CHAPTER ELEVEN
THE ROOT OF BITTERNESS

Each heart knows its own bitterness.
(Proverbs 14:10)

Bitterness arises in our hearts when we do not trust in the sovereign rule of God in our lives.
(Jerry Bridges, *The Pursuit of Holiness*)

The story is told that just before he began work on his famous painting *The Last Supper*, Leonardo da Vinci had a violent quarrel with a fellow painter. Apparently he was so enraged and bitter that he decided to paint the face of his enemy, the other painter, into the face of Judas and thus take his revenge by handing the man down in infamy and scorn to succeeding generations. The face of Judas was therefore one of the first he finished, and everyone could easily recognize it as the face of the painter with whom da Vinci had quarrelled.

When da Vinci came to paint the face of Jesus, apparently he could make no progress. Something seemed to be holding him back, frustrating his best efforts. At length he came to the conclusion that the thing frustrating him was the fact that he had painted his enemy into the face of Judas. He therefore painted out the face of Judas and began anew to paint the face of Jesus, this time with the success that the ages have acclaimed. In order to move forward it was necessary for da Vinci to get rid of the bitterness in his heart.

Nearly everyone has been hurt by the words or actions of another, and these wounds can leave you with lasting feelings of anger, bitterness or even vengeance. It is interesting to observe that people who are bitter seem to have an amazing memory for the tiniest detail, and they wallow in their resentment. If bitterness takes control of your life, it will become all-consuming and rob you of the joy in life.

In the previous chapter we looked at the topic of suffering and concluded that if we have the wrong perspective on suffering, this too can lead to a spirit of bitterness against God. The author and radio host Charles Swindoll writes, "Christians are called to respond to suffering in ways that mirror God's ongoing response to suffering revealed in the life, death and resurrection of Jesus…God does not promise freedom from suffering…but he does promise to give suffering a shape and context that are potentially transformative."[49]

In Ruth 1:1–21 there is a story of a woman who became so bitter that she changed her name to "bitter" to signify how she looked at life. There had been a famine in the land of Judah, so Elimelech and his wife, Naomi, took their two sons to the country of Moab to start a new life. While they lived there the sons grew up and married local women. However, disaster struck their home. Elimelech and his two sons died, and consequently Naomi and her two daughters-in-law were left as widows. Having no means of support, Naomi decided to return to her own people in Judah but wanted her daughters-in-law to stay in their own country and remarry. One decided to do so, but the other, named Ruth, refused, and she went to Judah with Naomi.

As they arrived in Bethlehem the town came out to meet them, and some of the women exclaimed "*Can this be Naomi?*" But Naomi replied, "*Don't call me Naomi…Call me Mara, because the Almighty has made my life very bitter. I went away full, but the LORD has brought me back empty. Why call me Naomi? The LORD has afflicted me; the Almighty has brought misfortune upon me*" (Ruth 1:19–21).

Bitterness can creep into our lives, and it can destroy us if we don't deal with it. It becomes like a seed that is planted in us. In the Bible there is the term "root of bitterness." The original use of the term comes from a warning Moses gave to the people of Israel. "*Make sure there is no man or woman, clan or tribe among you today whose heart turns away from the LORD our God to go and worship the gods of those nations; make sure there is no root among you that produces such bitter poison*" (Deuteronomy 29:18). What Moses was addressing was idolatry of the Israelites. They professed to follow God, but in reality they were worshipping other gods. This action was like a root that was spreading poison through the entire system, and in the end it would destroy the people.

The writer to the Hebrews picks up this theme in the life of the early church. He states, "*Make every effort to live in peace with all men and to be holy; without holiness no one will see the Lord. See to it that no one misses the grace of God and that no bitter root grows up to cause trouble and defile many*" (Hebrews 12:14–15).

Situations will arise whereby we have a choice to become bitter or better. It all depends upon how we choose to respond. As followers of Jesus our commitment to him must be more than simply words; it must be evident in how we live. When wronged it is easy to become bitter and want to get even; this is how many in our culture react. We are called to forgive, and if our behaviour speaks otherwise, the bitterness is like a poisonous root that will permeate all of our life.

If anyone could have been bitter about the circumstances of his early life it would be the Old Testament patriarch Joseph. However, he learned not to let the devastating circumstances of his life become a poisonous root destroying his life, his relationship with God and those who had wronged him.

Joseph was one of the 12 sons of Jacob. Of all his sons Jacob favoured Joseph, and such favouritism was detrimental to Joseph's relationship with his brothers. We read, "*When his brothers saw that their father loved him more than any of them, they hated him and could not speak a kind word to him*" (Genesis 37:4).

When Joseph was sent by his father, Jacob, to check on the welfare of his brothers who were grazing the flocks near Dothan, the brothers saw this as an opportunity to be rid of him. Their first plan was to kill him and tell their old father that his son had been killed by a wild animal. In the providence of God, Judah, one of the brothers, persuaded the others to sell him as a slave in Egypt. At least his life was spared.

In slavery in Egypt Joseph served in the house of Potiphar, the captain of the guard. Everything Joseph did pleased Potiphar, and eventually Joseph was put in charge of the entire household. The Bible tells us that God blessed the house of Potiphar because of Joseph (Genesis 39:5).

Potiphar's wife was attracted to Joseph, and she tried several times, unsuccessfully, to seduce him. When he rejected her advances, she ultimately accused him of rape, and Joseph landed in jail to spend the rest of his days as a prisoner. But Joseph was not forgotten. "*While Joseph was there in the prison, the LORD was with him; he showed him kindness and granted him favor in the eyes of the prison warden*" (Genesis 39:20–21).

In prison Joseph encountered the wine steward and the baker who served in Pharaoh's court, and they discovered that Joseph had the ability to interpret dreams. While Joseph was still languishing in prison, Pharaoh had two dreams that were perplexing to him, and no one could interpret them. The wine steward, who at that time had been released from prison and was serving again in Pharaoh's court, remembered Joseph and recommended him to Pharaoh.

Living, Dying, Living Forever

Through the interpretation of the dreams Joseph advised Pharaoh that there would be seven years of prosperity, followed by seven years of famine. He recommended that during the years of prosperity food should be stored in preparation for the years of famine. Not only did Pharaoh release Joseph from prison, but he placed him in charge of all operations and declared, "*Since God has made all this known to you, there is no one so discerning and wise as you. You shall be in charge of my palace, and all my people are to submit to your orders… I hereby put you in charge of the whole land of Egypt*" (Genesis 41:39–41). Life can change radically, from the prison to the palace in one day!

The seven years of famine were devastating, not only to the Egyptians but also to the surrounding countries. In Canaan where Joseph's family resided, they had no food, so their only course of action was to go to Egypt and buy some. When the sons of Jacob came to buy food, Joseph immediately recognized them, but they had no clue as to his true identity. Over the course of events Joseph's identity was made known to them, and eventually the entire family, including his elderly father, was reunited.

Joseph had been mistreated by his brothers. Now he was in a position of power and authority whereby he could seek revenge for all the harm they had done to him, but revenge was not in his heart. As Joseph reflected on life and all he had experienced, he looked at the big picture. To his brothers he said, "'*You intended to harm me, but God intended it for good to accomplish what is now being done, the saving of many lives…'* *And he reassured them and spoke kindly to them*" (Genesis 50:20–21).

This story has been told so that we might see the big picture. When injustice is done, we tend to see only the immediate events and not the way in which God is working on a grander scheme. When this happens it is easy to allow bitterness to take root, which manifests itself in an unforgiving spirit and a negative critical attitude. Joseph could have talked about the injustices and the pain he experienced, but he chose to see what God had done in and through his life. He did not allow a root of bitterness to develop; he saw the big picture. But there is more: his faith in God was not just a belief system but a relationship of trust lived out day after day after day.

The Old Testament prophet Jeremiah did everything God asked him to do, and it seems that in 40 years of ministry all he experienced was grief and persecution. Yet as he reflected on life he offered words of hope for all who struggle with hurt, pain and injustice: "*Because of the LORD 's great love we are not consumed, for his compassions never fail. They are new every morning; great is your faithfulness*" (Lamentations 3:22–23).

Have you experienced hurts and injustice and feel bitterness welling up in your spirit? Do you feel resentment toward others?

The following four questions may help you to discern if you have a root of bitterness.

1. When a certain person comes to mind, are you filled with resentment or bitterness towards him or her?

2. When another person experiences trouble or difficulty, do you ever think to yourself "They deserve it" or "I'm glad that it happened to them"?

3. Do you ever have thoughts about what you would like to do to another person to get even for the hurt they have caused you?

4. Do you ever try to get the support of others by speaking badly about another person?

If you want to be free from bitterness, you need to give your hurt and pain and any injustices you have experienced over to God. If you hang on to bitterness you will be filled with resentment, which, in the words of St. Augustine of Hippo, "is like taking poison and hoping the other person will die." In other words, bitterness will destroy you.

If we are honest there are times when we do enjoy holding things against others, but God tells us, "*Get rid of bitterness…Be kind and compassionate to one another, forgiving each other*" (Ephesians 4:31–32). Bitterness must go; if it doesn't, it will destroy your relationship with God, and it will alienate you from other people.

When you let go of the bitterness, there will still be situations that remind you of the painful event. Instead of reliving it over and over in your mind, begin to focus on what God has done and is doing in your life. The Psalmist said, "*Bless the LORD, O my soul, and all that is within me, bless his holy name! Bless the LORD, O my soul, and forget not all his benefits*" (Psalm 103:1–2, ESV).

Remember, God is using all of our circumstances in ways we might not fully comprehend at the moment. He asks us to trust him completely and to know he is working out all circumstances for our good. Joseph did not realize when he was sold as a slave, then wrongly accused by Potiphar's wife and imprisoned, that God was working through these situations to save a nation and restore a family. But he was!

If you hold bitterness in your heart, let it go. See what God is going to do through it all. Remember, God sees the big picture!

Reflections

1. Ask God to make known to you any bitterness that may be in your heart. Take a few moments to be still and listen. Sometimes we do not know our hearts very well; we will even deny the obvious. The prophet wrote, "*The heart is deceitful above all things*" (Jeremiah 17:9).

_____

_____

_____

_____

2. Read Ephesians 4:31–32. Instead of being bitter toward another, ask God to reveal to you practical ways to show kindness, compassion and forgiveness toward a person who has offended, criticized, belittled or shamed you.

_____

_____

_____

_____

3. Stop focusing on your hurts, and think about the blessings God has brought into your life. Remember the words of the Psalmist: "*Bless the LORD, O my soul, and forget not all his benefits*" (Psalm 103:2, ESV). Take some time to list the blessings you have received, and then express your gratitude to Almighty God.

_____

_____

_____

_____

4. Memorize these words, and let them touch your heart as well as your mind: "*Because of the LORD 's great love we are not consumed, for his compassions never fail. They are new every morning; great is your faithfulness*" (Lamentations 3:21).

CHAPTER TWELVE

WHEN YOUR HEART BREAKS

There is…a time to weep.
(Ecclesiastes 3:1–4)

Tears, idle tears, I know what they mean,
Tears from the depths of some divine despair
Rise in the heart, and gather to the eyes,
In looking on the happy autumn fields,
And thinking of the days that are no more.
(Alfred Tennyson)

Living, Dying, Living Forever

Ella Wheeler Wilcox's famous quote "Laugh and the world laughs with you; weep and you weep alone" is about something that has been experienced by many people. People are willing to celebrate with us in our moments of joy but often find it hard to enter into our pain and struggle. What do we do with our tears?

In Scripture we discover that many people wept. Jesus wept at the grave of Lazarus. Job wept over the death of his children. Jeremiah was described as the weeping prophet as he anguished over the sins of the nation.

Sadness is part of life, and all of us know sorrow and grief through the losses we have experienced. It may be the loss of our job, the loss of our home, the loss of our reputation, the loss of our health or the loss of a loved one. When we experience loss, how do we give expression to what is happening to us? Can we share it with others? Will they understand and empathize with us? Does God even care about us?

Sometimes in our pain we wonder if God has abandoned us. The psalmist David wrote, "*How long, O LORD? Will you forget me forever? How long will you hide your face from me?*" (Psalm 13:1). The psalmist Asaph cried out, "*Will the Lord reject forever? Will he never show his favor again? Has his unfailing love vanished forever? Has his promise failed for all time?*" (Psalm 77:7–8). This sense of God's abandonment has been described as the dark night of the soul.

The biblical scholar Bruce Demarest wrote about Mother Theresa, who ministered for almost 50 years among the poor and dying on the streets in India. During most of that time she lived in what is referred to as the dark night of the soul. This she described as "a profound interior suffering, lack of sensible consolation, spiritual dryness, an apparent absence of God from life, and, at the same time, a painful longing for him." But during this time Mother Theresa came to believe that God was using this experience to purify her imperfections, deepen her love for Jesus and intensify her compassion for the poor. Thus she was able to say, "I have come to love the darkness, for I believe now that it is a part of a very, very small part of Jesus' darkness and pain on earth."[50]

How do we give expression to our pain, suffering and loss? In the Bible the prayers of lament helps us bring all of our struggles to God. Lament not only provides us with a language to express what is happening but also is a realistic expression of our pain, anger and sadness.

Psalm 6 is an example of a person crying out to God in the midst of sickness and death.

> *O LORD, do not rebuke me in your anger or discipline me in your wrath.*
> *Be merciful to me, LORD, for I am faint; O LORD, heal me, for my bones*
> *are in agony. My soul is in anguish. How long, O LORD, how long? Turn,*

O L<small>ORD</small>, and deliver me; save me because of your unfailing love. No one remembers you when he is dead. Who praises you from the grave? I am worn out from groaning; all night long I flood my bed with weeping and drench my couch with tears. My eyes grow weak with sorrow; they fail because of all my foes. (Psalm 6:1–7)

In this psalm the writer openly expresses his pain to God. However, there is an element of hope that begins to shine through: "*The L<small>ORD</small> has heard my cry for mercy; the L<small>ORD</small> accepts my prayer*" (Psalm 6:9).

What is important to understand is that in the midst of all the suffering the Psalmist knows God is present, even though he might not sense his presence.

There are many other examples of lament in the Bible. Perhaps you will identify with some of them.

Solomon, the writer of Ecclesiastes, laments over the meaninglessness of life: "'*Meaningless! Meaningless!' says the Teacher. 'Utterly meaningless! Everything is meaningless*" (Ecclesiastes 1:2).

The prophet Habakkuk does not understand why God is acting in a way that seems to be inconsistent with his character. He yells,

How long, O L<small>ORD</small>, must I call for help, but you do not listen? Or cry out to you, "Violence!" but you do not save? Why do you make me look at injustice? Why do you tolerate wrong? Destruction and violence are before me; there is strife, and conflict abounds. Therefore the law is paralyzed, and justice never prevails. The wicked hem in the righteous, so that justice is perverted. (Habakkuk 1:2–4)

Matthew records the lament of those who lost their children through death. When Jesus was born, Magi who came from the east approached Herod and asked where was the one who was born king of the Jews. This greatly upset Herod, for he perceived this "king" to be a rival for his throne. When they discovered that according to prophecy the child was to be born in Bethlehem, Herod asked the Magi to come and inform him of the place when they found the child. Being warned in a dream not to go back to Herod, they returned home by another route. We are told, "*When Herod realized that he had been out-witted by the Magi, he was furious, and he gave orders to kill all the boys in Bethlehem and its vicinity who were two years old and under, in accordance with the time he had learned from the Magi*" (Matthew 2:16).

Living, Dying, Living Forever

Can you imagine the pain and anguish of these parents who had their little ones taken from them and their lives snuffed out? Jeremiah had prophesied it years before, and Matthew recorded the lament: "*A voice is heard in Ramah, weeping and great mourning, Rachel weeping for her children and refusing to be comforted, because they are no more*" (Matthew 2:18).

Jesus was not unfamiliar with pain and suffering. The prophet Isaiah wrote,

> *He was despised and rejected by men, a man of sorrows, and familiar with suffering. Like one from whom men hide their faces he was despised, and we esteemed him not. Surely he took up our infirmities and carried our sorrows, yet we considered him stricken by God, smitten by him, and afflicted. But he was pierced for our transgressions, he was crushed for our iniquities; the punishment that brought us peace was upon him, and by his wounds we are healed.* (Isaiah 53:3–5)

The ultimate expression of lament was when Jesus was dying on the cross. We are told that "*At the ninth hour Jesus cried out in a loud voice, 'Eloi, Eloi, lama sabachthani?'—which means, 'My God, my God, why have you forsaken me?'*" (Mark 15:34). For three hours Jesus never said a word, but now this cry comes from the depths of his being. They were familiar words. They were words of a prayer he learned from childhood, words from Psalm 22, written by David. Why did Jesus pray this prayer as he was dying? Why did he believe he was forsaken by God?

We do not know when Jesus became aware of his mission, but when he was eight days old his parents presented him at the temple, and old Simeon took the child in his arms blessed him. Then Simeon said to Mary, "*This child is destined to cause the falling and rising of many in Israel, and to be a sign that will be spoken against, so that the thoughts of many hearts will be revealed. And a sword will pierce your own soul too*" (Luke 2:34–35). "*A sword will pierce your own soul*"; what could this mean?

At 12 years of age Jesus knew that he had to do the Father's work, and steadfastly he set out to do all that the Father commanded. Toward the end of his ministry, when Jesus knew he was about to be arrested and ultimately be put to death, he prayed, "*Father, if you are willing, take this cup from me; yet not my will, but yours be done*" (Luke 22:42).

Jesus desired that this bitter cup be removed, but the Father said no. His suffering was the will of the Father. As he died, Jesus cried out, "*My God, my God, why have you forsaken me?*" (Mark 15:34).

The theologian Allen Verhey views this prayer as the climax to the horrors of his death:

Death made its power felt in Gethsemane when the disciples failed…to keep vigil with Christ. It made its power felt when one disciple betrayed him, when another denied him, when they all forsook him and fled. It made its power felt when it seemed God had forsaken him, when the council of his own people condemned him and when Pilate sentenced him. It made its power felt when the soldiers tortured him. It made its power felt in crucifixion…But the greatest threat was the threat of alienation from God and on that cross death made its power felt when it seemed God had forsaken him.[51]

Jesus went to the cross to bear the punishment for our sins, and that punishment meant he was forsaken by the Father. The musician and author Michael Card writes,

When he lamented "Why have you forsaken me?" Jesus voiced all our laments. The heartbreaking truth is…God did forsake him. Suspended over the "Place of the Skull" held there by Roman nails, hung the God—forsaken God. Their eternal unity impossibly broken, because God could not look upon the sin that Jesus became.[52]

Because he was forsaken it means that we will never have to be forsaken by God. Michael Card writes,

Jesus was forsaken for our sakes when he took upon himself all our sins upon which God, with his pure eyes, could not look. For the only time in all eternity, God looked away from his son. Jesus experienced the hell of his hidden face, so that if we come to him, we will never be separated from God's presence.[53]

The apostle Paul, writing to the church in Rome, asked and answered this question: "*Who shall separate us from the love of Christ?… in all these things we are more than conquerors through him who loved us…nor anything else in all creation, will be able to separate us from the love of God that is in Christ Jesus our Lord*" (Romans 8:35–39).

As we struggle with the questions of suffering and pain and death, we realize there is no definitive answer. In our pain, brokenness, confusion, doubt, sadness and the seeming absence of God, we pray our prayers of lament. Even if we do not understand everything that is happening and we do not sense the presence of God with us, we choose to trust his promise that he is with us forever. We will never weep alone. He is Immanuel, "God with us."

Reflections

1. What pain or suffering are you experiencing? Does God seem to be silent or not interested in what you are going through? Do you ever feel as if you are forsaken by God?

_____

_____

_____

_____

2. Psalm 6
Read verses 1–7. This is a very honest expression of what the writer is experiencing. What are some of the things that he declares?

_____

_____

_____

_____

3. Does he see any help at all? If so, what is it?

_____

_____

_____

_____

4. Write out your own lament to God. Remember, this is the language that expresses our grief, so be as honest as possible.

_____

_____

_____

_____

Prayer: This prayer, taken from Psalm 13, may be a prayer you can offer to God as you pray through your own struggles. Allow yourself to feel and experience the pain or sadness or difficulties you are going through.

Psalm 13

O God, sometimes You seem so far away.
I cannot in this moment sense Your presence
Or feel Your power.
This darkness about me is stifling.
This depression is suffocating.

How long, O God, do I have to live in this world?
O God, how long?
Break into this black night, O God;
Fill in this vast emptiness.
Enter into my conflict
Lest I fall never to rise again.

I continue to trust in Your ever-present love.
I shall again discover true joy
In my relationship with You.
I will proclaim Your praises, my Lord,
For You will never let me go.[54]

ADMITTING THE TRUTH ABOUT YOURSELF

He who conceals his sins does not prosper, but whoever confesses and renounces them finds mercy.
(Proverbs 28:13)

In confession…we open our lives to healing, reconciling, restoring, uplifting grace of Him who loves us in spite of what we are.
(Louis Cassels)

Many are familiar with the age-old adage "Confession is good for the soul." It sounds good, but we struggle because we know that confession is difficult to do. In life we make choices that are hurtful and destructive to our relationships with God and with others. Let's face it: it is not easy to admit that we are not the people we would like to be, let alone the people God would have us be. We are more than aware of our shortcomings and failures. So we need to make a choice: we confess our sins, or we continue to live under the guise of concealing our wrongdoings from ourselves and God and pretend that everything is OK.

However, when people hear the word "confession" it conjures up different images, such as entering the confessional and declaring their sins to a priest, an act some are familiar with and others would deem irrelevant. For some, confession implies what they do on their deathbed to insure there are no loose ends and that their life is in order before they die.

In 1936, the Polish virtuoso Hall Haberman had his Stradivarius violin stolen from his dressing room at Carnegie Hall by Julian Altman, a nightclub musician. In 1985, 49 years after the theft, Altman, now very ill and dying from cancer, confessed to his wife that he had stolen the violin, but it wasn't until 1987 (2 years later) that she returned the Stradivarius to Lloyds of London in return for $263,000 finder's fee. Today the violinist Joshua Bell owns the violin. Altman confessed to his wife what he did, but did he ever confess to God?[55]

If we choose not to acknowledge and confess our sins, then we never receive the mercy and forgiveness of God. The writer of Proverbs states, "*He who conceals his sins does not prosper, but whoever confesses and renounces them finds mercy*" (Proverbs 28:13). There are times when we would rather cover up our sins or minimize what we have done. We do this in different ways, such as rationalizing our behaviour, denying the seriousness of the issue or simply offering prayers in the form of a general confession, "forgive my sins and wrongdoings," yet never mentioning the specific things we have done.

The Psalmist paints a picture that contrasts one who confesses his sins with one who attempts to conceal or cover up what he has done:

> *Blessed is he whose transgressions are forgiven, whose sins are covered. Blessed is the man whose sin the LORD does not count against him and in whose spirit is no deceit. When I kept silent, my bones wasted away through my groaning all day long. For day and night your hand was heavy upon me; my strength was sapped as in the heat of summer. Then I acknowledged my sin to you and did not cover up my iniquity. I said, "I will confess my transgressions to the LORD"—and you forgave the guilt of my sin.* (Psalm 32:1–5)

It is not difficult to identify with these words. There have been occasions when we tried to hide the reality of our sins from ourselves, from others and from God. The consequence of such action is that we cannot know the joy of forgiveness and the restoration of our relationships with others and with God.

Some wonder why we need to confess our sins to God. Doesn't God already know the state of our hearts? Absolutely! God knows our secret thoughts, motives and even our deceptions, but confession of sin to God is not an act of informing God of what we have done; rather, it is the acknowledgement of what he already knows. We were created by

God to be in a right relationship with him, but the reality of sin separates us from him. In order for the relationship to be restored, our sins must be forgiven. The apostle John writes, "*If we claim to be without sin, we deceive ourselves and the truth is not in us. If we confess our sins, he is faithful and just and will forgive us our sins and purify us from all unrighteousness*" (1 John 1:8–9). If we want to be in a right relationship with God, we must be transparent before him and seek his mercy and forgiveness.

Some will ask, "What if I have sinned against others? Do I still need to confess to God?" We need to understand that sin is a transgression or failure to be or to do what God wants of us. We have failed to attain God's absolute standard of keeping his moral law. The Bible expositor and minister John Stott states, "Even if our sins are an offence to our fellow man, because we hate them or envy them or are rude or unkind to them, they are also a sin against God because they are a breach of his great commandment. 'You shall love your neighbour as yourself.'"[56]

To illustrate his point Stott cites an example from the life of David, the king of Israel, when he had an affair with Bathsheba, the wife of Uriah, a faithful soldier in David's army. He writes,

> [David] saw her bathing and was attracted by her beauty, lusted after her, took her for himself, had a child by her, and arranged for her husband to be killed in battle. One after another he broke four of the last five commandments: he coveted, he stole, he committed adultery, he murdered. And yet, when through the ministry of the prophet Nathan he was brought to repentance, he cried: "Against Thee, Thee only have I sinned and done evil in Thy sight" (Psalm 51:4) this is not a denial that he had sinned against Bathsheba, against her lawful husband, and against the whole nation of which he was king; but it is a recognition that all sins are first and foremost a defiance of the holy laws of God.[57]

When we confess our sins we must first come before a holy God whose laws we have violated, but we also need to confess to those we have injured or hurt. This might sound straightforward, but in reality it is difficult to do. Our pride gets in the way, and we don't want to humble ourselves to seek the forgiveness of another, or perhaps we wonder if they will actually forgive us for what we have done. Reflecting on this, the Lutheran pastor Dietrich Bonhoeffer wrote, "Since this humiliation is so painful, we would rather bypass it and think it is enough to confess to God…Confession of sin to another person is an act of discipleship to the cross. By confession we gain freedom from pride of flesh and reason."[58]

We can't expect to have a close relationship with God if our relationship with a brother or sister is broken. Jesus declared, "*If you are offering your gift at the altar and there* remember that your brother has something against you, leave your gift there in front of the altar. First go and be reconciled to your brother; then come and offer your gift" (Matthew 5:23–24). The principle is, go and seek to restore the relationship, regardless of how you might feel, and then you can come and worship God.

We confess our sins to God and to those we have wronged, but do we ever confess our wrongdoings in the presence of another? This has been termed "auricular confession," which simply means "confession of sins in the presence of a priest or minister." John writes, "*If you forgive the sins of any, they are forgiven them; if you retain the sins of any, they are retained*" (John 20:23, NKJV).

There are some people who have privately confessed their sins to God but have no sense of forgiveness. Bonhoeffer wrote,

> A man who confesses his sins in the presence of a brother knows that he is no longer alone by himself; he experiences the presence of God in the reality of the other person. As long as I am by myself in the confession of sins, everything remains in the dark, but in the presence of a brother the sin has been brought into the light.[59]

This form of confession is unfamiliar to many. As a minister, many times congregants have come to me to "confess" what they have done against God and against others. When I hear their stories, what do I say? "Your sins are forgiven" or "Don't worry about this" or "Go and tell this to God" or "I absolve you of all wrongdoing"? In fact, what I tell them to do is what the Scriptures tell us to do. I simply proclaim the words of assurance of pardon, that God has forgiven. I cannot forgive the sins of anyone; only God can do that. However, we have been given the authority to declare God's words of forgiveness. "*If we confess our sins, he is faithful and just and will forgive us our sins and purify us from all unrighteousness*" (1 John 1:9). The person is invited to receive the grace and mercy of God, and in his name they are declared forgiven. This ministry is not reserved for only ordained clergy but is given to all the people of God as we embrace the priesthood of all believers.

In order for our relationships to be healthy and growing, it is important for us to engage in a process of regular self-examination. Years ago, St. Ignatius developed a prayer form that enabled people to reflect on life in such a manner that they would not let their days go by unnoticed. This prayer is based on Psalm 139, which is an expression of the truths that God is the searcher of every heart and that there are no secrets hidden from him. For some this might be a fearful thought.

Marjorie Thompson, the director of Pathways Center for Spiritual Formation, encourages us to pursue this prayer of self-examination for two reasons. The first is so that we know

God loves us and that, no matter what we have done, none of our sins can erase his love. The second reason is so that we recognize the brokenness in our relationship with God. There is nothing we can do to fix ourselves, so we turn to face God, who alone can bring about the needed change in our life.

Thompson states, "Bathed in God's love, we can see clearly and non defensively all the destructive patterns of our false self: the facades we have hidden behind, the excuses we have relied on to avoid taking responsibility, our habits of deception and control, our failure to love God, others, or ourselves adequately."[60]

To engage in this prayer, there are a couple of steps that can easily be followed. You may need to adapt it in a manner that best suits you.

Begin your prayer by recalling the presence of God. "*In him we live and move and have our being*" (Acts 17:28). Each day is filled with a variety of events and experiences. Some days are relaxed, while others are filled with tension. Some days are productive, while others are challenging. In all circumstances of life, God is present. So we begin by simply slowing down and reflecting on God's presence. We know theologically that he is always present, but in prayer we place ourselves in his presence in an attentive manner. God the Father loves and cares for you in the deepest possible way. Through Jesus Christ you know of your significance and value to God, and the Holy Spirit leads you into all truth so that you may know God more fully. In this prayer begin by asking God to reveal himself to you.

The second step is to ask the Holy Spirit to help you. "*When he, the Spirit of truth, comes, he will guide you into all truth*" (John 16:13). Ask the Holy Spirit to give you sensitivity as you look over your day. The Spirit gives you freedom to look at your life in a way that is neither destructive nor condemnatory. Ask that you will be able to learn and grow as you reflect on issues God brings to your conscious awareness, and through this you will deepen your knowledge of self and your relationship with God.

The third step is to review your day. "*Examine yourselves to see whether you are in the faith; test yourselves. Do you not realize that Christ Jesus is in you…?*" (2 Corinthians 13:5). Recall the events of the day to see the way you reacted. Did you actively seek the presence of God in all you were doing? Are there habits you have gotten into that hinder relationships? Where did you fail today? Are there people you have hurt or offended? These simple questions help you to be more focused as you bring Christ into every aspect of your life.

The final step is an honest, transparent conversation with God. Here you may be led to ask God for forgiveness. Remember, his desire is that you experience healing grace and forgiveness. Be resolved to move forward in a different manner as you acknowledge that you are a recipient of God's mercy. Remember "*If anyone is in Christ, he is a new creation; the old has gone, the new has come!*" (2 Corinthians 5:17).[61]

Some have found it helpful as they do this exercise to focus on various questions that enable them to stay focused. Some people use these exercises by praying through the Ten Commandments or the Beatitudes. You might consider taking one commandment or one beatitude each day and using this as your prayer focus to examine your life before God and your relationships with others.

The Beatitudes (Matthew 5:3–10)

> "*Blessed are the poor in spirit, for theirs is the kingdom of heaven. Blessed are those who mourn, for they will be comforted. Blessed are the meek, for they will inherit the earth. Blessed are those who hunger and thirst for righteousness, for they will be filled. Blessed are the merciful, for they will be shown mercy. Blessed are the pure in heart, for they will see God. Blessed are the peacemakers, for they will be called sons of God. 10 Blessed are those who are persecuted because of righteousness, for theirs is the kingdom of heaven.*"

The Ten Commandments (Exodus 20:3–17)

> "*You shall have no other gods before me...You shall not make for yourself an idol... You shall not bow down to them or worship them...You shall not misuse the name of the LORD your God... Remember the Sabbath day by keeping it holy... Honor your father and your mother...You shall not murder. You shall not commit adultery. You shall not steal. You shall not give false testimony against your neighbor. You shall not covet.*"

Where are you today? What are the issues you are facing? Some realize their lives are passing quickly, and there is the need to repair broken relationships. Others think, "I have all the time in the world." Today is the day we need to live to the fullest. God alone holds the future, and what he desires is that we experience the abundant life he offers, one day at a time. So move forward, be a risk taker, don't let pride get in the way, and seek to be in right relationship with God and with others. When that happens, everything falls into place. Remember, all you will take with you after death is the relationship you have with God and with one another. It is good to have this sorted out now.

Reflections

1. Take some time to make a life review. Ask God to reveal to you any areas of your life that need to be confessed to him. Write it down, and then slowly and deliberately tell God each detail. Ask God for forgiveness. Read these words: "*If we confess our sins, he is faithful and just and will forgive us our sins and purify us from all unrighteousness*" (1 John 1:9). Now declare that God has forgiven you.

_____

_____

_____

_____

2. If God brings to mind any person you have hurt or offended, determine to seek their forgiveness. You may need to call them, write a letter, send an email or, if possible, speak to them face to face.

_____

_____

_____

_____

3. You may be prompted to ask your close family members or a dear friend to make known to you any blind spots you have. Their response can guide your confession.

_____

_____

_____

_____

4. God may have revealed to you some area of your life that needs to be confessed in the presence of another, such as your pastor or a trusted Christian friend. Make sure they understand the nature of this ministry and are prepared to come and speak God's words into your life.

5. Prayer of Confession

> Gracious God, our sins are too heavy to carry, too real to hide, and too deep to undo. Forgive what our lips tremble to name, what our hearts can no longer bear, and what has become for us a consuming fire of judgment. Set us free from a past that we cannot change; open us to a future in which we can be changed; and grant us grace to grow more and more in your likeness and image, through Jesus Christ, the light of the world.
> Amen.[62]

Living, Dying, Living Forever

The LORD is compassionate and gracious, slow to anger, abounding in love. He will not always accuse, nor will he harbor his anger forever; he does not treat us as our sins deserve or repay us according to our iniquities. For as high as the heavens are above the earth, so great is his love for those who fear him; as far as the east is from the west, so far has he removed our transgressions from us. (Psalm 103:8–12)

CHAPTER FOURTEEN
FORGIVE ONE ANOTHER

If we confess our sins, he is faithful and just and will forgive us our sins and purify us from all unrighteousness.
(1 John 1:9)

To be a Christian means to forgive the inexcusable because God has forgiven the inexcusable in you.
(C. S. Lewis)[63]

Some years ago, Simon Wiesenthal wrote a book called *The Sunflower*.[64] While imprisoned in a Nazi concentration camp, Wiesenthal was taken one day from his work detail to the bedside of a dying member of the notorious SS. Haunted by the crimes in which he had participated, the soldier wanted to confess to and obtain absolution from a Jew before he died. Faced with the choice between justice and compassion, silence and truth, Wiesenthal said nothing and walked out of the room. Years after the war ended, Wiesenthal often thought about that incident and wondered if he had done the right thing.

In our relationships with God and with others, one of the most important factors is the grace of forgiveness. Author Ken Boa states, "There is no sin so great that God will not forgive, but there is no sin so small that it does not need to be forgiven."[65] There is a prayer Jesus taught that is very familiar. Take a moment to read it and think about the words:

> "'Our Father in heaven, hallowed be your name, your kingdom come, your will be done on earth as it is in heaven. Give us today our daily bread. Forgive us our debts, as we also have forgiven our debtors. And lead us not into temptation, but deliver us from the evil one.' For if you forgive men when they sin against you, your heavenly Father will also forgive you. But if you do not forgive men their sins, your Father will not forgive your sins." (Matthew 6:9–15)

This prayer, though familiar, challenges us to consider what we are actually praying. When it comes to forgiveness, do we really mean "*Forgive us our debts, as we also have forgiven our debtors*"? When we ask God to forgive us, he actually eradicates the sin. In the Old Testament we read, "*As far as the east is from the west, so far has he removed our transgressions from us*" (Psalm 103:12). And what is amazing is that the Lord "*will forgive [our] wickedness and will remember [our] sins no more*" (Jeremiah 31:34).

It is wonderful to realize that God's forgiveness is able to restore our relationship with him, but he also desires the broken relationships with others to be restored. We know there are relationship where we have been hurt and where we have caused hurt to others. We want to be forgiven by God and by others, but at the same time there are situations where we do not find it easy to forgive those who have wronged us.

The prayer Jesus taught contains a conditional request, "God, forgive me as I forgive others." Jesus expands on this by adding "*For if you forgive men when they sin against you, your heavenly Father will also forgive you. But if you do not forgive men their sins, your Father will not forgive your sins.*" Richard Foster explains: "It is not that God begrudges his forgiveness nor is it hard to get God to forgive that we must demonstrate good faith by showing how well we can first forgive others. No, not at all! It is simply that by the very nature of the created order we must give in order to receive."[66]

Jesus told a great story to illustrate the point. Peter the disciple came to Jesus one day and asked a question about forgiveness, a question many still ask. In essence the question was "How many times do I forgive someone who has wronged me?" Peter, being somewhat generous, suggested seven times, but to his surprise Jesus said seventy times seven, which is a Hebraism meaning you forgive without setting limits.

Jesus proceeded to tell the story of a king who wanted to settle accounts with his servants. One servant owed millions of dollars. According to the laws of the day, he and his family could be sold as slaves in order for the king to recover some of his losses. The man begged for mercy, asking for more time to be able to repay the debt. To his great shock, the king cancelled the debt...a debt he could never have repaid if he worked for his entire life.

The servant went out from the presence of the king. Can you imagine the joy in his heart? Along the way he ran into another servant who happened to owe him a few dollars. He demanded that this man pay up immediately. This servant asked for a bit more time to repay the debt...a debt that could be repaid, but his plea fell on deaf ears, and ultimately he was thrown into prison until the debt was repaid.

When the king heard of this action, he was furious and ordered the first servant thrown into prison. To that servant the king posed a question, a question we all need to consider: "*I canceled all that debt of yours because you begged me to. Shouldn't you have had mercy on your fellow servant just as I had on you?*" Then Jesus makes this final comment: "*This is how my heavenly Father will treat each of you unless you forgive your brother from your heart*" (Matthew 18:32–35).

Reflecting on this story, theologian Allen Verhey comments,

> The gospel of God's forgiveness is...both gracious and demanding. To receive such grace is to be enabled and permitted to live—and to die—in accord with it. It is not that we earn forgiveness by being forgiving ourselves. It is no calculating "works righteousness," not even at the ending of our lives. It is rather that we are made new, made part of transforming humanity in which kindness, compassion, mutual love, and forgiveness are the rule.[67]

The apostle Paul knew about forgiveness. He referred to himself as the chief of sinners. He was a devout Jew who persecuted the early church and had the power and authority to have them imprisoned and put to death. When he encountered the grace and forgiveness of God, he was a changed person. He no longer sought revenge but offered forgiveness and mercy to all. Later he would write to the Christians at Colossae, "*As God's chosen people, holy and dearly loved, clothe yourselves with compassion, kindness, humility, gentleness and patience. Bear with each other and forgive whatever grievances you may have against one another. Forgive as the Lord forgave you*" (Colossians 3:12–13).

We are to forgive in direct proportion to the forgiveness we have received from God, which seems to be limitless.

One evening Jesus was invited to a dinner party hosted by Simon, a Pharisee. A woman who had a questionable reputation heard that Jesus was going to be at the house of Simon and came and stood behind Jesus. Weeping, she poured very expensive perfume on his feet. Simon was horrified by such actions! Simon thought to himself, if Jesus was a prophet, he would know that the woman who touched him was a sinner.

Jesus turned to Simon and said,

> "*Do you see this woman? I came into your house. You did not give me any water for my feet, but she wet my feet with her tears and wiped them with her hair. You did not give me a kiss, but this woman, from the time I entered, has not stopped kissing my feet. You did not put oil on my head, but she has poured perfume on my feet. Therefore, I tell you, her many sins have been forgiven—for she loved much. But he who has been forgiven little loves little.*" (Luke 7:44–47)

Perhaps we find it hard to forgive because we don't feel forgiven. As we experience the grace and love of God toward us we become more loving and gracious to others, and we are willing to forgive. If we have bitterness in our hearts, we need to bring that to God to experience his forgiveness and healing. If we do not forgive others who have hurt or wounded us, we will become bitter, and our resentment toward them will grow, simply because it has the ability to keep the emotions caused by the hurt alive. This will eventually destroy us if we do not deal with it.

At the end of his life Jesus prayed from the cross, "*Father, forgive them, for they do not know what they are doing*" (Luke 23:34). Stephen, the first Christian martyr, uttered words of forgiveness as he was dying: "*Lord, do not hold this sin against them*" (Acts 7:60). Our willingness and readiness to forgive bears witness to the power of God working in our lives. Allen Verhey comments,

> The readiness to forgive is a mark of dying well and faithfully. It is resistance to the rule of sin and death in the face of death. Death and sin make their power felt in the surrendering of relationships, in alienation from those we love and ought to love. Death and sin make their power felt in the nursing of grievances, in the desire for revenge, in the self serving insistence that justice be done and that any offence against us be punished. The human condition is one long story of keeping score of offences…To die well and faithfully is not to take grudges to the grave. It is not to nurse little grievances while we lie dying. It is to forgive. It is to be reconciled with those we counted as enemies…this is a common life formed by the grace of God.[68]

There are many different perspectives about the nature of forgiveness. Richard Foster in his book entitled *Prayer* says there are four things forgiveness is not.[69] First, forgiveness does not mean we will not feel the hurt caused by the wrongdoing. In some instances it can take a long time for the pain from the hurt to subside and the memory of the event to lose its power.

Second, forgiveness does not mean we will forget what happened and that we try to excuse the person or smooth things over. This does not get to the core of the problem. Some believe in the adage "forgive and forget," but if you think about what this means, it implies you would have lost your capacity for recall and consequently you would not even remember why you were forgiving the person.

When the Bible declares that God remembers our sins no more (Jeremiah 31:34), it does not mean that God had a lapse in memory; rather, it refers to the fact that he treats us as if we had not sinned. The theologian R. C Sproul comments, "The forgetting of God is a relational forgetting. That is he remembers my sin no more against me. When God forgives me of my sin he doesn't hold it against me. He bears no grudges. He harbors no lingering hostility. My relationship with him is totally and completely restored."

Third, forgiveness does not mean we pretend the offence did not matter. If it did not matter, then why are we so hurt by and angry about what has taken place? Often the greatest hurt has been caused by those who love us the most. If this is not dealt with, the relationship will suffer greatly.

Finally, forgiveness does not mean things will be the same as they were before the offence occurred. There can be forgiveness with reconciliation and forgiveness without reconciliation. For reconciliation to occur, both the offender and the offended must want the relationship to continue. If not, then you must part ways. At times this is the only way we can survive.[70]

So what is forgiveness? Forgiveness is that I surrender my right as I perceive it to get even or to hurt you back. It means that I release those who have hurt me by offering forgiveness. Without this act, bitterness and resentment will control my life. Ken Boa writes,

> To forgive as we have been forgiven by God is an act of faith, since it means that we are releasing the right to resentment and that we entrust justice to God rather than seek it ourselves *"Do not take revenge, my friends, but leave room for God's wrath, for it is written: 'It is mine to avenge; I will repay,'" says the Lord"* (Romans 12:19). To forgive is to act on the truth that it is only God and not we who can change another person.[71]

We need to be clear: forgiveness is not based on how I feel; it is an act of the will motivated by obedience to God and his command to forgive. So, for our good and the good of those who have wronged us, we must forgive.

Are you willing to forgive those who have wronged you? It is a choice that only you can make, because it is a decision to treat someone who has hurt and offended you with mercy and grace.

There is a risk involved when we forgive. The risk is that I am very vulnerable and the offender may hurt me again. When I have forgiven someone and he or she hurts me again and again, the hurt is greater each time. Psychologist David Benner comments,

> While there are risks to forgiveness, there are also risks to withholding forgiveness. And these risks are greater. The risk of being unforgiving is a life of chronic bitterness and hatred. This is a terminal condition, one that involves the destruction of body, soul, and spirit. The chances of damage to ourselves from withholding forgiveness are extremely high and we must, therefore, be careful to never underestimate these risks. The chances of a subsequent hurt at the hands of the one who hurt me are not to be ignored but are usually lower than the chances of hurt to myself if I withhold forgiveness. On this basis…forgiveness is always the better risk.[72]

Ask God for the grace to forgive even as you have experienced his forgiveness.

Reflections

1. Take a few moments in quietness and reflect on this question: "How have I experienced the forgiveness of God?" Write out your thoughts.

_____
_____
_____
_____

2. Do you have any feelings of resentment or bitterness toward anyone who has hurt you? Name the person and what they have done, entrusting to God the feelings of hurt and anger that it has brought to you. Now, before God, choose to forgive them. "God, I choose to forgive _____ for _____

_____
_____
_____

I now surrender any thought of getting even, and I commit this person to your care.

Do this for each specific person and situation that God brings to your awareness.

3. Meditate on these words: "*Blessed are the merciful, for they shall receive mercy*" (Matthew 5:7, ESV). If anything comes to your mind or is stirred in your spirit as you meditate on this verse, note it down and then offer it to God.

_____

_____

_____

_____

4. I invite you to offer this prayer of forgiveness and reflect on the issues you are dealing with on a personal level:

      Lift us, Lord,
      Out of darkness into light,
      Out of despair into hope.

      Lift us, Lord,
      Out of sadness into joy,
      Out of failure into trust.

      Lift us, Lord,
      Out of anger into forgiveness,
      Out of pride into freedom.
      Amen.[73]

5. Conclude by praying the Lord's Prayer:

      Our Father in heaven
      Hallowed be your name.
      Your kingdom come
      Your will be done
      On earth as in heaven.
      Give us today our daily bread
      Forgive us our debts
      As we have forgiven our debtors.
      Lead us not into temptation but deliver us from evil
      For the kingdom and the power and the glory are Yours
      Forever.
      Amen.

CHAPTER FIFTEEN
LIVING WITH HOPE

May the God of hope fill you with all joy and peace as you trust in him, so that you may overflow with hope by the power of the Holy Spirit.
(Romans 15:13)

To live without hope is to cease to live.
(Dostoevsky)

We all need to have hope, for without it life becomes unbearable and we are left with despair. Ben Patterson in his book *The Grand Essentials* tells a story about an S-4 submarine that was rammed off the coast of Massachusetts. It sank immediately. The entire crew was trapped in a prison house of death. Every effort was made to rescue the crew, but all attempts failed.

Near the end of the ordeal, a deep sea diver, who was doing everything in his power to find a way for the crew's rescue, thought he heard a tapping in the steel wall off the sunken sub. He placed his helmet up against the side of the vessel, and he realized it was Morse code. He attached himself to the side, and he spelled out in his mind the message being tapped from within. It was repeating the same question. The question was "Is…there…any…hope?"

Hope is really important to our human existence as we face the challenges and trials of life. Charles Swindoll suggests hope is a wonderful gift from God:

- When we are trapped in a tunnel of misery, hope points to the light at the end.
- When we are overworked and exhausted, hope gives us fresh energy.
- When we are discouraged, hope lifts our spirits.
- When we are tempted to quit, hope keeps us going.
- When we lose our way and confusion blurs the destination, hope dulls the edge of panic.
- When we struggle with a crippling disease or a lingering illness, hope helps us persevere beyond the pain.
- When we fear the worst, hope brings reminders that God is still in control.
- When we must endure the consequences of bad decisions, hope fuels our recovery.
- When we are forced to sit back and wait, hope gives us the patience to trust.
- When we feel rejected and abandoned, hope reminds us we're not alone…we'll make it.
- When we say our final farewell to someone we love, hope in life beyond gets us through our grief.[74]

Hope is essential for all of us. Recently I had the opportunity to hear a lecture given by William Hauben, who was a Holocaust survivor. At the end of World War II when he was liberated from the Ebensee Concentration Camp, he completed three years of intensive vocal studies in Verona, Italy. Then he moved to the United States, where he completed studies for the cantorate at the Cantor's Institute of the College of Jewish Studies in Chicago, Illinois. As I listened to his amazing story I wondered how was it possible to not give up and lose hope of survival.

The secret of his survival was that William Hauben believed that God had a purpose for him, and that purpose was to be a witness. He was to be a living witness to tell the world of the atrocities that occurred so that this would never happen again to anyone, any-where. Then he quoted these words:

How can I repay the Lord for all his gifts to me?
I will raise the cup of deliverance,
And invoke the Lord by name.

I will pay my vows to the Lord in the presence of all his people.
Grievous in the sight of the Lord is the death of his faithful.
I am your servant, born of your maidservant;
You have released me from bondage.
To you will I bring an offering and invoke the Lord by name.
My vows to the Lord will I pay in the presence of all his people
In the courts of the house of the Lord
In the midst of Jerusalem, hallelujah. (Psalm 116:12–19)

Much of what William Hauben said was similar to what the famous physician Dr. Victor Frankel, also a Holocaust survivor of the death camps, believed. Frankel realized that when people lost hope they simply gave up and died. Hope not only enhanced life but gave people a totally different perspective.

So, what is hope? For some it is simply wishful thinking or an expression of a desire we have. The pastor and author Lloyd Ogilvie suggests,

> Human perceptions of what we hope for usually involves wishful think-
> ing. We all have wished for our selves, for other people and for the
> future. These wishes are the result of our human desires-what we have
> evaluated would be best for us and others, or for some situation.
> Sometimes we try to wish things into existence. At the same time we
> attempt to wish away other things.[75]

As one who has been a lifelong fan of the Toronto Maple Leafs, I begin every season saying, "I hope they win the cup this year." I hope they will, but in reality, I don't think it will happen. It has been over 40 years since they won the trophy! Hope in this instance is simply trying to be optimistic.

A biblical understanding of hope is quite different. Actually, it is a gift God gives to us. No matter what circumstance I am facing, I have hope, because I believe in the fact that God is sovereign over every situation that happens in life and that he is faithful according to his promises. Therefore I choose to trust him for everything in life, because I know his desire for each person is only that which is good. There are numerous examples of this throughout Scripture.

Years ago God spoke to the prophet Jeremiah words of great promise and hope: "'*For I know the plans I have for you,' declares the Lord, 'plans to prosper you and not to harm you, plans to give you hope and a future'*" (Jeremiah 29:11).

It is important to understand the context of this promise of hope and a future. The Jewish people were living in exile in Babylon. The people longed to be able to go home, so some of the prophets amongst them tried to give them some hope, but it was false hope. They told the people that the exile would not last long and they would soon be able to return home. God spoke to Jeremiah and told him to tell the people that this word of hope by the prophets was not true. In fact, they would remain in exile for 70 years. In the meantime they were to settle down, build houses, plant gardens, get married and have children. One more thing—they were to pray for the peace and prosperity of the city, because if there was peace and if the city prospered, they too would reap the benefits.

When the 70 years were completed, the Lord would return them to their land. The promise of "*plans to prosper you and not to harm you, plans to give you hope and a future*" was intended to bring hope, but it would be fulfilled according to the sovereign plan of God. Would they trust God?

These people living in exile had a great history that could remind them of the faithfulness of God, if they would only recall what God had done. Years before they were living in exile, the Israelites were being attacked by the Philistine army and were terrified of what would happen to them. The prophet Samuel cried to the Lord on behalf of the people, and God intervened by causing such a powerful thunderstorm that the Philistine army was thrown into chaos and routed by the Israelites. When it was all over, Samuel took a large stone and erected it as a monument and named it Ebenezer, meaning "*Thus far has the LORD helped us*" (1 Samuel 7:12). These people would face other challenges, but this monument was intended to be a constant reminder of the faithfulness of God, and when you know that God is faithful, hope abounds.

In the early church the apostle Paul was aware that many situations in life could lead people to despair. Yet he was filled with hope. To the church in Corinth he wrote,

> *We do not want you to be uninformed, brothers, about the hardships*
> *we suffered in the province of Asia. We were under great pressure, far*
> *beyond our ability to endure, so that we despaired even of life. Indeed,*
> *in our hearts we felt the sentence of death. But this happened that we*
> *might not rely on ourselves but on God, who raises the dead. He has*
> *delivered us from such a deadly peril, and he will deliver us. On him*
> *we have set our hope that he will continue to deliver us.* (2 Corinthians
> 1:8–10)

Although Paul wondered if they might die, he chose to focus on the power and presence of Almighty God. Later he would write,

> *We do not lose heart. Though outwardly we are wasting away, yet*
> *inwardly we are being renewed day by day. For our light and momen-*
> *tary troubles are achieving for us an eternal glory that far outweighs*

them all. So we fix our eyes not on what is seen, but on what is unseen. For what is seen is temporary, but what is unseen is eternal. (2 Corinthians 4:16–18)

This became the perspective that gave him hope even while dying.

When death is imminent, people often have a different perspective on hope. From a psychological perspective, it's a type of hope that is changing and is somewhat limited. The psychologist Theresa Rando writes,

> Initially the hope is that the diagnosis will be proven incorrect. This changes upon confirmation of the diagnosis, to the hope that there will be a cure or some miracle that will enable the patient to escape death. Later this hope is transformed to a smaller scale and the patient hopes that life will be optimal, albeit limited (e.g., with the minimum of pain and disruption of life). Smaller hopes related to everyday life and activities…it is this hope that sustains the patient through suffering. When all hope becomes lost there is a psychological and then a physical surrender to the environment.[76]

We can understand this approach to hope, but if we are honest it is very fleeting, and in the end there is death. We recognize that death will happen to everyone, but as Christians we know that this is not the end of the story. Ultimately, our hope is not focused on getting better but on aligning our life with God's purposes for us. In spite of all that might happen to us, we do not need to despair. The apostle Paul wrote, "*We also rejoice in our sufferings, because we know that suffering produces perseverance; perseverance, character; and character, hope. And hope does not disappoint us, because God has poured out his love into our hearts by the Holy Spirit, whom he has given us*" (Romans 5:3–5).

We rejoice in the sufferings we experience, not because we enjoy suffering in some perverse manner, but because we recognize that God is using the situations and circumstances we encounter to build our character. We live in an environment where troubles are inevitable but not insurmountable. The suffering we experience is designed not to drive us from God but rather to draw us to him. This is possible because we have experienced the love of God being poured out in our hearts by the Holy Spirit. This relationship develops even through difficult circumstances whereby we begin to realize that what is most important in life is our relationship with God and that one day we will share in the glory of God.

The apostle Peter refers to this as a living hope. He states, "*Praise be to the God and Father of our Lord Jesus Christ! In his great mercy he has given us new birth into a living hope through the resurrection of Jesus Christ from the dead, and into an inheritance that can never perish, spoil or fade—kept in heaven for you*" (1 Peter 1:3–4). As difficult as life might be, we can know that this is not the end of the story. Our ultimate hope is that one day we will be with God. God has a place for us, and nothing can destroy it. Charles Swindoll writes,

> Who can mind the journey when the road leads home…So if you want to smile through your tears, if you want to rejoice through times of suffering, just keep reminding yourself that as a Christian, what you are going through isn't the end of the story…it's simply the rough journey that leads to the right destination.[77]

This ultimate hope is based on the resurrection of Jesus from the dead. If God brought his Son back from the dead, we can have confidence that he will be able to help us through any situation we are facing. The psalmist wrote words of promise for pilgrims on the journey of life that have sustained the people of God over the ages: "*The LORD watches over you…The LORD will keep you from all harm—he will watch over your life; the LORD will watch over your coming and going both now and forevermore*" (Psalm 121:5, 7–8)

When it comes time for us to face our death, we realize that not even death can separate us from God, because we belong to him. The Heidelberg Confession poses the question "What is your only comfort in life and death?" The answer is "That I am not my own, but belong—body and soul—to my faithful Saviour Jesus Christ."

The greatest assurance we can have in life is that we belong to God. The apostle Paul wrote, "*If we live, we live to the Lord; and if we die, we die to the Lord. So, whether we live or die, we belong to the Lord*" (Romans 14:8). This certainty enables us to live confidently day by day, no matter what. If you are somewhat fearful about life and what it holds for you, remember, God will keep you. He called you to be his, and he will never let go of you. Paul wrote, "*He who began a good work in you will carry it on to completion until the day of Christ Jesus*" (Philippians 1:6).

J. I. Packer reminds us,

> What matters supremely, therefore, is not, in the last analysis, the fact that I know God, but the larger fact which underlies it—that he knows me. I am graven on the palms of his hands. I am never out of his mind. All my knowledge of him depends on his sustained initiative in knowing me. I know him because he first knew me, and continues to know me. He knows me as a friend, one who loves me; and there is no moment when his eye is off me, or his attention distracted from me, and no moment, therefore, when his care falters. This is

momentous knowledge. There is unspeakable comfort…in knowing that God is constantly taking knowledge of me and watching over me for my good.[78]

Is this the hope you have as you face each day? The journey of life has many challenges. The children of Israel lived in exile; they faced numerous enemies; and the early Christians suffered great hardships, but through it all they found hope in God, who was faithful to his promises. They had monuments erected to remember what God had done. His promises for us are still the same. He is "*the same yesterday and today and forever*" (Hebrews 13:8). He is the one who does not change; therefore his word is sure and true.

What we begin to realize is that what is really important in life is not all that we have accomplished or acquired; rather it is the relationship we have developed with God. He is the source of our hope, knowing that one day we will share in the glory of God. John the Apostle wrote, "*Now we are children of God, and what we will be has not yet been made known. But we know that when he appears, we shall be like him, for we shall see him as he is*" (1 John 3:2).

Imagine that! One day we shall see God face to face. That is our hope.

Reflections

1. Read and meditate on these words from Psalm 121:

> *I look up to the hills, but where does my help come from?*
> *My help comes from the LORD, who made heaven and earth.*
> *He will not let you be defeated. He who guards you will never sleep…*
> *The LORD guards you.*
> *The LORD is the shade that protects you from the sun.*
> *The sun cannot hurt you during the day,*
> *and the moon cannot hurt you at night.*
> *The LORD will protect you from all dangers; he will guard your life.*
> *The LORD will guard you as you come and go, both now and forever.*
> (Psalm 121:1–3, 5–8, NCV)

2. Take some time to think about your circumstances. How does this passage speak hope in the promises God has given?

_____

_____

_____

_____

3. Read the following prayer:

> I look to you for my help and protection in this uncertain world. You protect me from evil and preserve my soul. When I suffer pain and loss, even then I know that you will use it for my ultimate good by drawing me ever closer to you. My hope is centred on you and your ever present care.[79]
> Amen.

4. Memorize the following verse: "'For I know the plans I have for you,' declares the LORD, 'plans to prosper you and not to harm you, plans to give you hope and a future'" (Jeremiah 29:11).

CHAPTER SIXTEEN
LEAVING A LEGACY

You, however, know all about my teaching, my way of life, my purpose, faith, patience, love, endurance, persecutions, sufferings—what kinds of things happened to me…But as for you, continue in what you have learned and have become convinced of, because you know those from whom you learned it.
(2 Timothy 3:10–14)

The greatest use of life is to spend it for something that will outlast it.
(William James)

I was sitting on a beach in southern Florida when a family next to me began building a sand sculpture. They worked hard for over two hours, and in the end there emerged from the sand a beautiful mermaid, complete with hair made of seaweed. Upon my return to the beach the next day, the mermaid was gone. Either the tide took away the sand sculpture or, I suspect, someone walked all over it, and the mermaid returned to grains of sand scattered over the beach.

For many people, I suspect, life is like that. We work hard and expend great amounts of energy, but in the end we wonder what has been significant and what will last. We ask, "Have I done anything of significance? Will I leave a legacy that will last?"

For many the legacy they leave is related to what they have done. The narrator of the book of Ecclesiastes has much to say about this. This narrator, referred to as the "philosopher" or the "teacher," is quite skeptical about this legacy. He approaches life from three perspectives.

The first perspective that the philosopher takes is that life will be meaningful through wisdom and learning. When this is not fulfilling, he pursues pleasure, and then he attempts to find purpose through various achievements attained by hard work. At the end of it all he concludes, "*So I hated life, because the work that is done under the sun was grievous to me. All of it is meaningless, a chasing after the wind*" (Ecclesiastes 2:17).

Why does he come to such a conclusion? The author and Presbyterian pastor Timothy Keller provides an interesting perspective:

> Nothing is more satisfying than a sense that through our work we have accomplished some lasting achievement. But the Philosopher startles us by arguing that even if you are one of the few people who breaks through and accomplishes all you hope for, it's all for nothing, for in the end there are no lasting achievements…Whether quickly or slowly, all the results of our toil will be wiped away by history…everything and every accomplishment under the sun will be ground to dust in the end—even civilization itself. All work, even the most historic, will eventually be forgotten and its impact totally neutralized.[80]

There is a wonderful story in the Gospels that reveals what is important and how we ought to invest our lives so that we have a lasting legacy. There were two brothers who were concerned about making it rich. They were left an inheritance, and one brother felt he was not going to get a fair share, something that many are familiar with if they have ever had to settle an estate. This brother wanted Jesus to be the arbiter of their dispute, hoping that somehow he would get a fair deal.

Jesus began by telling them to be careful about becoming greedy, because there are more important things in life than possessions. To emphasize the point, he told them a parable about a man who had done very well; in fact, he was accumulating wealth so quickly that he had to build larger buildings to house all that he had. Finally he thought, "I have achieved my goal in life," which was a life of ease, and to eat, drink and be merry was the measurement of his success. His entire life was focused on himself, and he thought *Life does not get any better than this.*

That night he died. He would not be able to enjoy all he had worked so hard to acquire; in fact, his possession would go to someone else. That was it!

In making a judgment about this man's life and the values that he operated from, God said that this man was a "*fool*" (Luke 12:20). Imagine being called by God a fool…a person who lacks common sense. Yet that is exactly what this man was. He invested his life in that which would not last forever. Then Jesus declared, "*This is how it will be with anyone who stores up things for himself but is not rich toward God*" (Luke 12:21). All of his investments were temporary; they would not stand the test of time. Leaving behind a lot of money was the legacy of this man, but he was not rich toward God.

What does it mean to be rich toward God? The author and pastor Lloyd Ogilvie suggests that "Richness with God begins in a relationship with him whereby we experience God's love and forgiveness without measure. Our richness toward God grows as we surrender the direction, goals and purposes of our life…and the passion of our life becomes seeking and doing the will of God."[81]

Such an individual was a man called Elijah, who left a legacy that would last. Elijah the Prophet was called by God to stand against the mainstream of his day. He confronted kings, queens and false prophets. He endured drought, famine and constant harassment, yet he remained faithful to God.

One day, after a particularly difficult experience when Elijah felt as if he was the only person left who was faithful to God, the Lord gave him his next assignment. He was to go to the Desert of Damascus and anoint Hazael as king of Aram, Jehu as king of Israel, and Elisha as his own replacement. In other words, Elisha was to become the next prophet. Elijah had to face the reality that this younger man would take over for him, and he did exactly as God asked him.

Elijah came down from the mountain where God spoke to him and saw Elisha plowing in a field. He came up to the young man, and without saying a word he took off his cloak and placed it on the shoulders of Elisha. Immediately Elisha left everything behind and followed him. In some versions of the Bible the cloak is referred to as a mantle. The author John Ortberg comments,

Living, Dying, Living Forever

Today when we talk about a mantle of responsibility or a mantle of leadership getting passed on it comes from this story. In a visible way, Elijah is saying to Elisha, "I am inviting you to follow me and learn from me. I want to walk with you and teach you. I want to have you watch what I do and then see how God can also work in and through your life." In a real sense Elijah is saying "I want to pass the flame to you. I want to give you the spiritual legacy God has given to me. I want your flame to burn brighter, and one day you will lead as the prophet in Israel without me even being at your side."[82]

So the two men walked together, and over the years Elijah mentored the young man. Toward the end of his life, when Elijah knew he was dying, he turned to his companion, Elisha, and asked him, *"What can I do for you before I am taken from you?"* What a difficult question to answer. But Elisha replied, *"Let me inherit a double portion of your spirit"* (2 Kings 2:9). At first glance this might sound a bit greedy; however, we need to understand that in biblical times this is what is referred to as "inheritance language." To ask for a double portion is to ask to be someone's heir. The firstborn son always received a double portion, for his responsibility through life was to look after his parent. Elisha was spiritually Elijah's firstborn son. Ortberg explains the request in this manner:

> Elisha is saying "Elijah, I've watched your life, I've seen your ministry. I've witnessed your devotion and the difference you've made. I've seen how Israel is a different place because of your ministry. The power of Baal worship has been broken because of your devotion and courage. I want to continue in following in your steps, even after you are gone."[83]

What an amazing legacy Elijah left.

All of us want to leave a legacy that will last. What is more important, the stuff we leave behind or the legacy that we have influenced the lives of the next generation? The philosopher Pericles stated, "What you leave behind is not what is engraved in stone monuments, but what is woven into the lives of others."

Take some time to examine your life. What is your focus? Are you investing in what will last? If we look at the culture, we must admit that many are investing in that which will not survive the test of time. Jesus said,

> *"Do not store up for yourselves treasures on earth, where moth and rust destroy, and where thieves break in and steal. But store up for yourselves treasures in heaven, where moth and rust do not destroy, and where thieves do not break in and steal. For where your treasure is, there your heart will be also"* (Matthew 6:19–21).

Gathering up stuff is not enough cause by which to structure your life. There is no long-term security; moths will destroy, things will rust out, thieves will steal. Jesus tells us to invest in that which will last forever.

However, there are many people who simply worry about things…what they will eat, what they will wear, what they will drink. It consumes their lives. We are to do one thing: "*Seek first the kingdom of God and his righteousness*" (Matthew 6:33, ESV). In other words, we desire first and foremost the reign and rule of God in our lives, and this will result in right living or, as Jesus called it, abundant life. We will have our priorities in the right place.

Jesus expanded on this when asked to summarize the important things in life. He said, "*Love the Lord your God with all your heart and with all your soul and with all your mind and with all your strength…Love your neighbor as yourself*" (Mark 12:30–31). What will last forever is your relationship with God and the relationships you have developed with others.

The theologian John Swinton writes, "Life in all of its fullness relates to living our lives in ways that reveal our love for God, self and one another in all things and at all times, including times of suffering and death…what is definitive of abundant life is the desire to love God in all things and at all times."[84]

Abundant life in our consumer-driven culture is all about the stuff we have accumulated or hope to have. On the tombstone of the "rich man," an appropriate epitaph that sums up his approach to life would read "He who has the most toys when he dies wins."

Today we can begin to live in such a way that we will leave a lasting legacy for those who come after us. What is important is not that we leave a huge bank account or property or other assets but rather that we have built into the lives of those whom God has placed in our path during our journey here on earth. It may be our sons and daughters or our grandchildren or people we work with or a class of students we teach. These are the people God is asking us to invest our lives in, and so we pass on the mantle, much like Elijah did with Elisha. When we do this we become channels of God's blessings, and thus we bless others.

Celebrate every encounter with the people God brings into your life, and remember, you are leaving with them that which is most important…a legacy.

Reflections

1. Read the story Jesus told of the man who built up his portfolio (Luke 12:16–21). As you read this story, enter into it as fully as possible. Be the man who is acquiring all the wealth.

2. How is your story like the man in the parable? What would Jesus say to you?

_____

_____

_____

_____

3. Who are the people who built a legacy into your life? What did they do?

_____

_____

_____

_____

4. What type of legacy would you like to leave? What are you doing to leave a lasting legacy?

_____

_____

_____

_____

5. Take a few moments to think about your life. How have you influenced others? Are there people who come to mind whom you desire to be a positive influence to? Who are they? What do you think you are to do?

_____

_____

_____

_____

6. The following prayer was offered by the apostle Paul for his friends in the city of Philippi. I encourage you to offer it as your prayer this day, thinking of particular individuals who are significant in your life.

This is my prayer: that your love may abound more and more in knowledge and depth of insight, so that you may be able to discern what is best and may be pure and blameless until the day of Christ, filled with the fruit of righteousness that comes through Jesus Christ—to the glory and praise of God. (Philippians 1:9–11)

CHAPTER SEVENTEEN

YOU ARE IN GOOD HANDS

The steadfast love of the LORD never ceases.
(Lamentations 3:22, ESV)

He is no fool who gives up what he cannot keep to gain what he cannot lose.
(Jim Elliot)[85]

Safety issues are a concern for all of us. Since 9/11 the world has implemented numerous safety and security measures. Travelling by airplane takes an extra hour to go through security checks, and if we see an unattended piece of luggage in a public setting, authorities are alerted. Telemarketers try to sell us home security devices to protect our property, we childproof our homes so our children will not get hurt, and we tell them not to talk to strangers. All of this is an attempt to protect and keep safe those we love.

Are you safe and secure in your relationship with God? John Ortberg in the book *Love Beyond Reason* tells a story based on the children's movie *The Bear* that reflects the relationship we have with God.

It is the saga of a tiny bear cub whose mother dies. The cub survives, but his long term chances are nil. Then the unexpected happens. The little cub gets more or less adopted by an enormous Kodiak. This giant is always watching over the cub. He protects it from a mountain lion who has been stalking him. He teaches the cub how to be a bear. Everything the father bear does the cub imitates: he waddles in the stream and stabs at fish like the daddy bear, he stands on two hind legs and scratches his back against a tree as he has seen his father do. This cub is going to live.

One day they get separated. The little bear can't see his father anywhere. The mountain lion has never forgotten the cub and now finally sees his opportunity. He comes swiftly, silently, face to face with the cub; he is about to spring. The little bear does what he has seen his father do: he rears up on his hind legs, lifts his paws, and tries to growl fiercely, but the best he can manage is a frightened squeak. The mountain lion is not convinced. Both the cub and his attacker know he is about to die.

Suddenly the mountain lion's face registers a look of fear. He stops snarling, turns and slinks away.

The cub is surprised watching this unfold. Could his growl have worked so well? Then we see what the cub could not see. Behind the little bear is the great Kodiak, standing on his hind legs, massive body poised to save his son with a single swipe.

Big paws. Fierce growl.

Then we know. That little bear had nothing to worry about. The cub could not see or hear him, but the father was there all the time. That forest was a perfectly safe place for the little cub to be. The father could be trusted, even when he seemed to be absent.[86]

It is a wonderful children's story, but what about us? Can we be secure in our relationship with God?

The most frequent promise that God gives to us is "I will be with you." When the children of Israel were making their way from Egypt to the Promised Land, a journey that took 40 years, God provided two symbols to remind them of his presence. By day there was a pillar of cloud, and by night there was a pillar of fire. Wherever they were, they could see these symbols and know that God was with them.

When the Son of God took on a human body and nature he was given the name Immanuel, which means "God is with us." Following the death of Jesus, his disciples were discouraged and wondered what would happen to them. On that resurrection Sunday two of them were walking on the road to Emmaus, and they encountered a third person, the risen victorious Christ. They did not recognize him immediately, but when he broke bread with them at the evening meal their eyes were opened. In fact they said, "*Did not our hearts burn within us while he talked to us on the road, while he opened to us the Scriptures?*" (Luke 24:32, ESV). The risen Christ was with them.

God is with us, and we are secure. One of the psalms of ascent sung by worshippers as they made their way to Jerusalem to worship reminds us not only of God's presence but that we are safe in his presence.

> I lift up my eyes to the hills—where does my help come from? My help comes from the LORD, the Maker of heaven and earth. He will not let your foot slip—he who watches over you will not slumber; indeed, he who watches over Israel will neither slumber nor sleep. The LORD watches over you—the LORD is your shade at your right hand; the sun will not harm you by day, nor the moon by night. The LORD will keep you from all harm—he will watch over your life; the LORD will watch over your coming and going both now and forevermore. (Psalm 121:1–8)

This does not mean that there will be no difficulties or challenges. The Bible is very realistic and clear that the people of God will face many challenges; however, none of this can separate us from God's love. This is the basis of our security.

Even at the end of our days we can rest secure in our relationship with God. The Psalmist wrote, "*Even though I walk through the valley of the shadow of death, I will fear no evil, for you are with me*" (Psalm 23:4). It is knowing the presence of God that gives us this sense of security, not only throughout our lifetime but also at the time of our dying.

Having a relationship with God is the source of our security. However, the first thing we need to grasp is that this relationship was initiated by God, not us. We did not seek out God; rather, he sought us and chose us to be his. The Bible tells us there is "*no one who seeks God*" (Romans 3:11). It is God alone who brings us to faith and repentance. Salvation is about God.

The most familiar verse in the Bible speaks about God's gift: "*God so loved the world that he gave his one and only Son, that whoever believes in him shall not perish but have eternal life*" (John 3:16). Jesus said, "*I have come that they may have life, and have it to the full*" (John 10:10).

If God gives us eternal life, does it not stand to reason that this relationship with him is forever? By definition, "eternal" implies that it never ends. Jesus, speaking in the Gospel of John, declares, "*My sheep listen to my voice; I know them, and they follow me. I give them eternal life, and they shall never perish; no one can snatch them out of my hand. My Father, who has given them to me, is greater than all; no one can snatch them out of my Father's hand. I and the Father are one*" (John 10:27–30). The late James Boice, pastor of Tenth Presbyterian Church in Philadelphia, commented,

Jesus says we are secure in his hand. We can imagine ourselves as a coin around which his fingers have folded. That is a secure position for any object, but especially for us, considering whose hand it is that holds us. But then lest we think that this is not enough, Jesus adds that the hand of God is over his hand so that we are enclosed in two hands. We are therefore doubly secure. If we feel insecure, we should be reminded that even when we are held in this manner, the Father and the Son still have two hands fee to defend us.[87]

The apostle Paul wrote, "*Being confident of this very thing, that He who has begun a good work in you will complete it until the day of Jesus Christ*" (Philippians 1:6, NKJV). God promises to finish what he started, and since he initiated the relationship with us, he is the one who will keep us in his love for all eternity.

As we will face challenges along the way, we need to be reminded that Jesus is our great high priest, the one who intercedes on our behalf before the presence of God to keep us safe. To be represented before God by a high priest and to be lost before we reach our heavenly home implies that our high priest is powerless and ineffective. Yet Jesus declared that all authority in heaven and earth had been given to him (Matthew 28:18). He will bring us safely to our heavenly home. We are secure.

But some will raise questions about those who appeared to have a relationship with God at one time but have distanced themselves from God. Did God not keep them safe and secure? Curtis Thomas offers several insights and states,

> The biblical teaching is that those who are genuine believers will never fall away from Christ. It is true that some may fall away from a temporary excitement over Christianity, or an emotional decision to follow Christ, or because of persecution, or the cares of the world become all important, or from a shallow commitment to a local church…The true child of God never falls away completely.[88]

The apostle John is very clear in explaining why some apparent believers fell away. "*They went out from us, but they were not of us; for if they had been of us, they would have continued with us; but they went out that they might be made manifest, that none of them were of us*" (1 John 2:19, NKJV). Their departure had a purpose in that it revealed that they were not true followers of the Lord Jesus Christ. They had some external manifestations, such as belonging to a church community, attending worship, knowing and reciting the creeds, praying and celebrating the sacraments. But it was all external. They were members of a local church, but they did not belong to Christ.

So the question remains, how do we know if we truly belong to the Lord? The biblical expositor John Stott clarifies this by stating, "'He who endures to the end shall be saved' (Mark 13:13) not because salvation is the reward of endurance, but because endurance is the hallmark of the saved."[89]

The true child of God is secure and delivered from the wrath of God to come at the Day of Judgment.

> *Since, therefore, we have now been justified by his blood, much more shall we be saved by him from the wrath of God. For if while we were enemies we were reconciled to God by the death of his Son, much more, now that we are reconciled, shall we be saved by his life (Romans 5:9–10, ESV).*

The apostle Paul tells us, "*Therefore, there is now no condemnation for those who are in Christ Jesus*" (Romans 8:1). God will never condemn us; we have been delivered from any judgment by the sacrifice of Christ on our behalf. Thus he concludes,

> *Who shall separate us from the love of Christ? Shall trouble or hardship or persecution or famine or nakedness or danger or sword?…No, in all these things we are more than conquerors through him who loved us. For I am convinced that neither death nor life, neither angels nor demons, neither the present nor the future, nor any powers, neither height nor depth, nor anything else in all creation, will be able to separate us from the love of God that is in Christ Jesus our Lord. (Romans 8:35–39)*

God has chosen you to be his child simply because he has chosen you. This is a relationship now that continues through the door of death into the next phase of eternal life. And the promise is that he will keep you safe!

> *Dear friends, build yourselves up in your most holy faith and pray in the Holy Spirit. Keep yourselves in God's love as you wait for the mercy of our Lord Jesus Christ to bring you to eternal life…To him who is able to keep you from falling and to present you before his glorious presence without fault and with great joy—to the only God our Savior be glory, majesty, power, and authority, through Jesus Christ our Lord, before all ages, now and forevermore! Amen. (Jude 1:20–21, 24–25)*

Reflections

1. Read Psalm 91, a psalm of security.

> *He who dwells in the shelter of the Most High will rest in the shadow of the Almighty. I will say of the* LORD, *"He is my refuge and my fortress, my God, in whom I trust."... "Because he loves me," says the* LORD, *"I will rescue him; I will protect him, for he acknowledges my name. He will call upon me, and I will answer him; I will be with him in trouble, I will deliver him and honor him. With long life will I satisfy him and show him my salvation."* (Psalm 91:1–2, 14–16)

2. Write out a short prayer that expresses the security you have in your relationship with God. Conclude by giving him thanks for this gift.

_____

_____

_____

_____

3. If there are times when you doubt your security in God, slowly and repeatedly offer this "breath prayer" until it resonates within your heart: *"He [Jesus] who began a good work in [me] will bring it to completion at the day of Jesus Christ"* (Philippians 1:6, ESV).

CHAPTER EIGHTEEN
GOING HOME

"I am going there to prepare a place for you… I will come back and take you to be with me that you also may be where I am."
(John 14:2–3)

Has this world been so kind to you that you should leave with regret? There are better things ahead than any we leave behind…Joy is the serious business of heaven.
(C. S. Lewis)[90]

Home for most people is a place of familiarity, comfort and security. We know it well, and it is an easy place to be. Moving to a new place can be challenging, since we leave behind all that is familiar and the security that brings and we venture into unfamiliar territory, not really sure what is ahead for us.

Living, Dying, Living Forever

This is true when we think about our death. What is ahead for us? All we have ever known is life here on earth, so what will our new home be like?

This was an issue Jesus' disciples faced. As he realized that the end of his ministry was near, he spoke of his impending death to the disciples. Naturally they were upset. What was going to happen to them? Would they be left alone and abandoned? And then the question that everyone wonders about, what is on the other side of death? Jesus addressed their concerns by speaking words of comfort to them:

> "*Do not let your hearts be troubled. Trust in God; trust also in me. In my Father's house are many rooms; if it were not so, I would have told you. I am going there to prepare a place for you. And if I go and prepare a place for you, I will come back and take you to be with me that you also may be where I am.*" (John 14:1–3)

Although Jesus was going away, there was no need for the disciples to feel afraid or anxious, because Jesus told them he was preparing a place for them, and he promised he will come back to them and he will take them to be with him.

Immediately we think of heaven as the place he is preparing for us. But where is heaven? The Bible actually makes reference to three heavens. The first heaven is what we refer to as the atmosphere (Genesis 7:11–12). The second heaven is a reference to the space in which the stars and planets are found (Genesis 1:14–17). The third heaven, which Paul spoke of, is none other than the home of God, the place Jesus said he is preparing for us (2 Corinthians 12). This heaven is eternal.[91]

In essence the promise Jesus spoke about to the disciples was that they would ultimately be with him. What he was asking them to do was to trust that what he was saying was true and at the time of death he would take them to the place he had prepared for them.

The Bible is filled with wonderful pictures and images of heaven. There are streets of gold, gates made of pearl, a river of life and trees for the healing of the nations. However one chooses to interpret these symbols, the key to understanding heaven is to realize it is not just a place, it is home.

A number of years ago the movie producer and director Stephen Spielberg produced the movie *E. T. the Extra-Terrestrial.* It was a story about a young boy, Elliot, who discovered an extraterrestrial who had been left behind by his fellow aliens. It eventually becomes clear that this creature, E. T., cannot survive the earth's atmosphere and must return to the planet from which he came. With the help of his new friend Elliot he is able to place a call to his planet, and eventually he is rescued. What is most touching about this story is the desire of this little creature to return home. As he is about to enter the spaceship and return to his planet, E. T.'s heart glows. He knows he is going home.

On a more serious note, Dr. Paul Tournier, a Swiss physician, in his book *A Place for You* addressed the need for a place called home. Tournier talked about a young man who had been born into an unhappy home and had lived his life with a sense of failure. As the young man explored his problems he came to the conclusion that the root of his struggles was simply based on the fact he was "looking for a place—for somewhere to be." This, concluded Tournier, is the desire of every person. We are looking for a place to belong.[92]

Although heaven is to be our new home, a place where there is no suffering no pain, no mourning and no death, the most important feature of heaven is that we will be with God in an unbroken relationship. The pastor and teacher John MacArthur states, "Simply put we are going to be with a Person as much as we are going to live in a place. The presence of Christ is what makes heaven, heaven. And perfect fellowship with God is the very essence of heaven."[93]

The Bible also tells us that in heaven we shall see God face to face, a reality that is impossible in this phase of life. Jesus said, "*Blessed are the pure in heart, for they will see God*" (Matthew 5:8).

We live each day looking forward to that certainty. The apostle John wrote, "*Dear friends, now we are children of God, and what we will be has not yet been made known. But we know that when he [Jesus] appears, we shall be like him, for we shall see him as he is*" (1 John 3:2).

As Jesus asked the disciples to trust him, so we are asked to trust him as well. The pastor and biblical expositor John Stott writes,

> In his grace Jesus goes further than a general command to trust him. He spells out in some detail why we may trust him and so not be afraid of death. First Jesus states he is going to prepare a place for us. With this in mind Jesus bids us think of death not as a leap into the dark unknown but as a journey to a prepared place.[94]

Jesus is promising not only to prepare a place for us but that he will also come and take us to be with him. Stephen, the first Christian martyr, as he was dying declared, "*I see heaven open and the Son of Man standing at the right hand of God*" (Acts 7:56). Stott states, "Jesus had risen from his throne in order…to welcome him."[95] This is most reassuring to all believers because we can grasp that dying is not something we need to fear but simply part of the process of going home to be with the Lord God Almighty. With this perspective we can look at death as a departure from this life to be with Christ. Stott reinforces this point:

> There is no need for us to speculate about the precise nature of heaven. We are assured on the authority of Jesus Christ that it is the home of his Father and ours...that this home is a prepared place...and that he himself will be there. What more do we need to know? To be certain where he is, there we shall be also should be enough to satisfy our curiosity and ally our fears.[96]

The homes we have established are important to all of us, but we need to realize that they are not permanent. Abraham the Patriarch was praised because he did not fix his hope on an earthly home (as important as that might be) but he looked for a heavenly home. The writer of Hebrews writes,

> *By faith he [Abraham] made his home in the promised land like a stranger in a foreign country; he lived in tents, as did Isaac and Jacob, who were heirs with him of the same promise. For he was looking forward to the city with foundations, whose architect and builder is God.* (Hebrews 11:9–10).

All of us need a home, one that is not temporal but eternal. This life is a journey, and we are pilgrims on our way to the home God has prepared for all who love him. One day we shall be home, and we will be in the Father's house. For now, we wait and trust.

Reflections

1. When you think about home, what are the pictures or images that are meaningful to you?

_____

_____

_____

_____

2. What are your thoughts about the life to come? What do you think it will be like? How do you know this?

_____

_____

_____

_____

3. Read Revelation 21:1–5. What words or phrases resonate with you? What is the most significant aspect of heaven that you find in this text? Why does it resonate with you?

_____

_____

_____

_____

4. Meditate on this text: "*Now the dwelling of God is with men, and he will live with them. They will be his people, and God himself will be with them and be their God*" (Revelation 21:3).

_____

_____

_____

_____

5. Offer this prayer:

"*Therefore, since we have a great high priest who has gone through the heavens, Jesus the Son of God…Let us then approach the throne of grace with confidence, so that we may receive mercy and find grace to help us in our time of need*" (Hebrews 4:14–16).

God of majesty and power, you led Jesus the Messiah through suffering into risen life and took him up to the glory of heaven. Now he rules over all things as Lord.

Help us to know his presence in all of life so that we will live with the assurance that one day we will be with him in glory.

O God, we look forward to the home you have prepared for us, a place where you dwell where there is no more sickness or suffering or sadness or death. All these things are gone, and you have made all things new.

Best of all, we know that one day we will be with you, and it is your presence that makes heaven our new home.

Amen.

CHAPTER NINETEEN
FINAL WORDS

"Lord Jesus, receive my spirit."
(Acts 7:59)
(Stephen, the first Christian martyr)

Money can't buy life.
(Bob Marley)

In July 1977, while seeking treatment for an injury sustained during a friendly football match, Bob Marley, the singer and songwriter and guitarist of the reggae band Bob Marley and the Wailers, was found to have acral lentiginous melanoma. He declined amputation of his toe, and the melanoma eventually spread to his brain and lungs. As his health declined and death was imminent, his final words to his son were "Money can't buy life." Bob Marley died at Cedars of Lebanon Hospital in Miami at the age of 36.

Last words are significant in that final words may be a summary of one's life and leave a lasting impression on those who hear them. David, the shepherd boy who became the most famous king of Israel, spoke his final words to his son Solomon:

> "I am about to go the way of all the earth," he said. "So be strong, show yourself a man, and observe what the LORD your God requires: Walk in his ways, and keep his decrees and commands, his laws and requirements, as written in the Law of Moses, so that you may prosper in all you do and wherever you go, and that the LORD may keep his promise to me: 'If your descendants watch how they live, and if they walk faithfully before me with all their heart and soul, you will never fail to have a man on the throne of Israel.'" (1 Kings 2:2–4)

Living, Dying, Living Forever

As he came to the end of his life, these final words of David reveal several things about life that he believed to be important. The first thing is that he accepted the reality of the inevitable. He was dying! He did not live with denial but had come to the place of acceptance (*"I am about to go the way of all the earth"*), and he wanted his son Solomon to know that reality. There are many who do not want to accept death, and thus they can't adequately prepare for their old age and eventual death. The reminder that one day we will die enables a person to truly live life to the full.

The second thing David spoke about was living life courageously. He wanted his son Solomon to be a courageous man. In his leadership position as the new king of Israel he would have to make many decisions, and some would not be popular and not always accepted by the general populace. David knew the burden of leadership with the challenges it entailed, and he wanted his son to understand that he must live courageously if he would be the man God wanted him to be.

The final message David left with Solomon was to obey all the commands and decrees of God. The evidence of devotion to God is seen in obedience to him. Jesus said, "*If anyone loves me, he will obey my teaching*" (John 14:23). It is not enough to articulate our beliefs; we must live out our devotion to God by following him with all our hearts.

David was aware that he had not done all these things perfectly, but he knew the blessings and benefits of following God wholeheartedly. This is what he wanted for his son more than anything else. Powerful words spoken at the end of life.

The most profound words spoken at the end of a life were those spoken by Jesus. These statements are commonly referred to as The Seven Last Words of Christ. As we briefly consider them, think about the implications for your life.

The First Word

> "*Father, forgive them, for they do not know what they are doing.*" (Luke 23:34)

The first words of Jesus are those of forgiveness. Luke is the only writer to record these words spoken by Jesus as he was crucified between two criminals. The two men knew they were guilty of the crimes they were being punished for but Jesus had done nothing wrong. Yet in his dying moments he offers words of forgiveness to those who were responsible for his execution. On a broader scale we realize that these words are words spoken for all people. Christ death was the punishment that would atone for our sin so that we might receive the forgiveness of God. In effect Jesus was saying, "Father, punish me and forgive them."

Reflection

As you listen to Jesus' words, how does it speak to your condition? Have you received the forgiveness offered by Jesus? Do you know the joy of being forgiven by Almighty God?

The Second Word

> "*Assuredly, I say to you, today you will be with Me in Paradise.*" (Luke 23:43, NKJV)

As Jesus hung on the cross between two criminals, the soldiers mocked him, and one of the criminals hurled insults at him: "*Aren't you the Christ? Save yourself and us!*" (Luke 23:39). However, the other criminal acknowledged that they were getting what they deserved but Jesus had done nothing wrong. Then he said, "*Jesus, remember me when you come into your kingdom*" (Luke 23:42). Jesus replied, "*I tell you the truth, today you will be with me in paradise*" (Luke 23:43).

Here is a man who knew that he had no hope apart from Jesus. He cried out to Jesus, and Jesus responded with mercy and grace. He told this man that he would be with him in paradise, or heaven. This criminal did not have a complete understanding of theology but discovered that a relationship with God begins by committing oneself to God in simple trust. The prayer is simply "Jesus, remember me." This account offers great hope to people. In the Bible this is the only "deathbed confession" recorded. There is only one so that we never lose hope, but there is only one so that we never become presumptuous.

Reflection

Have you committed yourself into the hands of God? Do have the certainly that you too will be with Jesus in paradise? The prayer is "Jesus, remember me."

The Third Word

> "*Dear woman, here is your son...Here is your mother.*" (John 19:26–28)

As he was dying, Jesus' mother and the disciple whom he loved, most likely John, were standing at the foot of the cross. Even though he was in agony he was concerned not for himself but for others. Knowing his responsibility to care for his mother, he committed her into the care of the "beloved" disciple. Jesus always thought about the needs of others.

Reflection

In what way have you been the recipient of Jesus' love and care? How can you offer this care to others that are a part of your life?

The Fourth Word

"*My God, my God, why have you abandoned me?*" (Mark 15:34, GWT)

These words from Psalm 22 were a way for Jesus to express the deep feelings in his heart. It was his lament. Though he cried out, we will never know the full extent of his suffering. What does it mean to be abandoned and rejected by God? The apostle Paul gives some insight: "*God made him who had no sin to be sin for us, so that in him we might become the righteousness of God*" (2 Corinthians 5:21).

Reflection

As you hear Jesus cry out these words, what does it mean to you? Take some time to meditate on the concept that Jesus was forsaken by God so you would never have to experience that reality.

The Fifth Word

"*I thirst.*" (John 19:28, ESV)

Crucifixion was a nasty business. The physical agony was unbearable. In the midst of his pain and suffering Jesus cried out, "*I thirst.*" It was a request for a drink of water, and in response the soldiers gave him "sour wine," a cheap drink that was common among the poor but also considered by some to be a way to help dull the pain.

This was not the first time Jesus asked for something to drink. Once while travelling from Judea to Galilee Jesus and the disciples had to travel through Samaria to reach their destination. When they reached the town of Sychar, Jesus sat down near a well while the disciples went to purchase some food. Meanwhile a woman came to the well to draw water, and Jesus asked her if she could draw some water from the well to give him a drink. This led to further conversations, which revealed deep needs in the woman's life. Jesus told her, "*Everyone who drinks this water [a reference to the well from which she was drawing the water] will be thirsty again, but whoever drinks the water I give will never thirst. Indeed, the water I give him will become in him a spring of water welling up to eternal life*" (John 4:13–14). This encounter with Jesus was transformational in the life of this woman.

As we hear these final words of Jesus, "*I thirst,*" we are reminded that Jesus offers the living water of eternal life.

Reflection

What do you thirst for? What is that intense desire in your life? How does Jesus meet that need?

The Sixth Word

> "*It is finished.*" (John 19:30)

When Jesus cried out these words, it meant on one level that his suffering was ended. There would be no more pain and suffering. But these words meant far more than the end of physical agony. When he declared, "*It is finished,*" it was a reference to the fact that he had completed his mission that the Father had given to him. Jesus said, "*For the Son of Man came to seek and to save the lost*" (Luke 19:10, ESV). His death was the atoning sacrifice to pay the penalty for all our sins. The penalty was paid. It is finished.

Reflection

Are you secure and confident in the work Jesus finished for you?

The Seventh Word

> "*Father, into your hands I entrust my spirit.*" (Luke 23:46, GWT)

These words were quoted from Psalm 31, which begins with a cry for help: "*I have taken refuge in you, O LORD. Never let me be put to shame. Save me because of your right-eousness… Into your hands I entrust my spirit*" (Psalm 31:1–5, GWT).

In this cry, Jesus trusts his future into the hands of the Father, knowing that ultimately he would be delivered. Death would not have the final word. When we place our life into the hands of Almighty God, we can be certain that death is not the end but that he will bring us into his glorious presence.

Reflection

Do you have the certainty that death is not victorious? Have you placed your life into the hands of the Father?

These final words of Jesus truly reflect his life and ministry. What will your final words reflect? Think about what you will say and to whom you will speak these important words. Perhaps you will be like David, who spoke words of wisdom and blessing to his son. As you reflect on your life, death and the life to come, remember, we are people of hope. The best is yet to be!

Aaronic Blessing

The LORD bless you and keep you; the LORD make his face shine upon you and be gracious to you; the LORD turn his face toward you and give you peace. (Numbers 6:24–26)

ENDNOTES

[1] Allen Verhey, *The Christian Art of Dying* (Grand Rapids: Eerdmans, 2011), 180.

[2] Rob Moll, *The Art of Dying* (Downers Grove: IVP, 2010), 56.

[3] Theresa Rando, *Grief, Dying and Death* (Champaign: Research Press, 1984), 1.

[4] Ken Boa, *Conformed to His Image* (Grand Rapids: Zondervan, 2001), 63.

[5] Ken Boa, *That I May Know Him* (Oregon: Multnomah Publishers, 1998), 57.

[6] Boa, *Conformed to His Image,* 462.

[7] Timothy Keller, *The Prodigal God* (New York: Dutton, 2008), 8.

[8] Joseph Stowell, *Coming Home* (Chicago: Moody Press, 1998), 33.

[9] Stowell, *Coming Home,* 48.

[10] Boa, *Conformed to His Image,* 31.

[11] Bruce Demarest, *Satisfy Your Soul* (Colorado Springs: Nav Press, 1999), 95.

[12] Boa, *Conformed to His Image,* 33.

[13] J. I. Packer, *Knowing God* (London: Hodder and Stoughton, 1973), 41.

[14] Richard Foster, *Celebration of Discipline* (New York: Harper Collins, 1998), 49.

[15] Richard Foster, *Prayer: Finding the Heart's True Home* (New York: Harper One, 1992), 147.

[16] Richard Foster, "Crucifying Our Will: Praying Through the Struggle to Let Go," *Knowing and Doing* (Fall 2005).

[17] Catherine Marshall, *Beyond Our Selves* (New York: McGraw-Hill, 1961), 94.

[18] Foster, *Celebration of Discipline,* 52.

[19] Søren Kierkegaard, "Journals IV A 164" (1843).

[20] "'You've got to find what you love,' Jobs says," Stanford Report (June 14, 2005), available at news.stanford.edu/news/2005/june15/jobs-061505.html.

[21] Eryn Sun, "Jeremy Lin's Favorite Bible Verse Reflects His Story of Perseverance," *Christian Post* (July 28, 2013).

[22] Verhey, *The Christian Art of Dying,* 340.

[23] Verhey, *The Christian Art of Dying,* 341.

[24] Charles Stanley, *How to Handle Adversity* (Nashville: Thomas Nelson Publishers, 1989), 146.

[25] Robert A. Emmons, *Gratitude Works!: A 21-Day Program for Creating Emotional Prosperity* (San Francisco: Josey Bass, 2013), 128.

[26] Darrell Bock, *The NIV Application Bible Commentary: Luke* (Grand Rapids: Zondervan, 1996), 445.

[27] Ken Boa, "Cultivating a Heart of Gratitude," *Ken Boa's Teaching Letters* (2006). Available at www.kenboa.org/page_print.php?link=/text_resources/teaching_letters/kens_teaching_letter/2090.

[28] Carolyn Hessel and Sulamith Ish-Kishor (eds.) *Blessed Is the Daughter* (Rockville: Schreiber, Shengold Publishing, 1999), 34.

[29] Boa, "Cultivating a Heart of Gratitude."

[30] Rando, *Grief, Death and Dying,* 233–237.

[31] Lloyd Ogilvie, *The Bush is Still Burning* (Waco: Word Books, 1980), 43.

[32] C.S. Lewis, *Mere Christianity* (New York: Harper Collins, 2009), 55.

[33] Lloyd Ogilvie, *Perfect Peace* (Oregon: Harvest House, 2001), 30.

[34] Rick Warren, *God's Power to Change Your Life* (Grand Rapids: Zondervan, 1998), 93.

[35] William Maddocks, *A Healing House of Prayer* (London: Hodder and Stoughton, 1987), 156

[36] Presbyterian Church USA, *Book of Common Worship* (Louisville: Westminster/John Knox, 1993), 148.

[37] Philip Yancy, "Faith and Doubt" (2009). Available at www.philipyancy.com/q-and-a-topics/faith and doubt.

[38] John Ortberg, *Faith And Doubt* (Grand Rapids: Zondervan, 2008), 137.

[39] Kerry Walters, *The Art of Dying and Living* (New York: Orbis Books, 2011), 22.

[40] Walter Brueggmann, *Awed to Heaven Rooted in Earth* (Minneapolis: Fortress Press, 2004), 54.

[41] Abigail Rian Evans, *Is God Still at the Bedside?* (Grand Rapids: Eerdmans, 2011), 224.

[42] R. C. Sproul, *Surprised by Suffering* (Wheaton: Tyndale House, 1988), 83.

[43] Evans, *Is God Still at the Bedside?,* 226.

[44] Alistair McGrath, *Suffering* (Reading: Cox and Wyman, 1992), 98.

[45] Alistair McGrath, *Intellectuals Don't Need God: Building Bridges to Faith Through Apologetics* (Grand Rapids: Zondervan, 1993), 106.

[46] McGrath, *Suffering,* 98.

[47] John Swinton and Richard Payne, eds., *Living Well and Dying Faithfully* (Grand Rapids: Eerdmans, 2009), 158.

[48] Evans, *Is God Still at the Bedside?,* 224.

[49] Charles Swindoll, *Hope Again* (Waco: Word Publishing, 1996), 108.

[50] Bruce Demarest, *Seasons of the Soul* (Downers Grove: IVP, 2009), 85.

[51] Verhey, *The Christian Art of Dying,* 226.

52 Michael Card, *A Sacred Sorrow* (Colorado Springs: Nav Press, 2005), 133.

53 Card, *A Sacred Sorrow,* 134.

54 Leslie Brandt, *Psalms-Now* (St. Louis: Concordia Publishing House, 1973), 23.

55 David J. Krajicek, "A Fiddle Found" (January 4, 2004). Available at www.joshuabell.com/story-his-violin.

56 John Stott, *Confess Your Sins* (London: Hodder and Stoughton, 1964), 20.

57 Stott, *Confess Your Sins,* 21.

58 Dietrich Bonhoeffer, *Spiritual Care* (Philadelphia: Harper and Row, 1985), 63.

59 Dietrich Bonhoeffer, *Life Together* (New York: Harper and Row, 1952), 116.

60 Marjorie Thompson, *Soul Feast* (Louisville: Westminister John Knox, 1995), 90–91.

61 David Sherbino, *Re:Connect: Spiritual Exercises to Develop Intimacy with God* (Toronto: Castle Quay Books 2013), 55–57.

62 *PCUSA Book of Common Worship* (Louisville: Westminister John Knox 1993), 88.

63 C. S. Lewis, *The Weight of Glory* (New York: Harper Collins, 2001), 183.

64 Simon Wiesenthal, *The Sunflower: On the Possibilities and Limits of Forgiveness* (New York: Schocken Books 1997).

65 Boa, *Conformed to His Image,* 49.

66 Foster, *Prayer: Finding the Heart's True Home,* 186.

67 Verhey, *The Christian Art of Dying,* 236.

68 Verhey, *The Christian Art of Dying,* 235.

69 Foster, *Prayer: Finding the Hearts True Home,* 187.

70 Foster, *Prayer: Finding the Hearts True Home,* 187.

71 Boa, *Conformed to His Image,* 50.

72 David Benner, *Healing Emotional Wounds* (Grand Rapids: Baker Book House, 1990), 116.

73 Ray Simpson, *Celtic Prayers for Today* (Buxhall: Kevin Mayhew, 2006), 51.

74 Swindoll, *Hope Again,* xi.

75 Lloyd Ogilvie, *The Greatest Counselor in the World* (Ann Arbor: Servant Publications, 1995), 94.

76 Rando, *Grief, Death and Dying,* 269.

77 Swindoll, *Hope Again,* 15.

78 Packer, *Knowing God,* 42.

79 Ken Boa, *Living Promises* (Nashville: Thomas Nelson, 2003), 19.

80 Timothy Keller, *Every Good Endeavor* (New York: Penguin Books 2012), 101.

81 Lloyd Ogilvie, *Autobiography of God* (Glendale: Regal Books, 1979), 135.

82 John Ortberg, *Pursuing Spiritual Authenticity* (Grand Rapids: Zondervan, 2004), 35.

83 Ortberg, *Pursuing Spiritual Authenticity,* 40.

84 Swinton and Payne, *Living Well and Dying Faithfully,* 6.

85 Elizabeth Elliot, *The Shadow of the Almighty* (New York: Harper Row 1958), 108.

86 John Ortberg, *Love Beyond Reason* (Grand Rapids: Zondervan, 1998), 166.

87 James Boice, *The Gospel of John* (Grand Rapids: Zondervan, 1985), 671.

88 Curtis Thomas, "Safe and Secure," available at http://www.ligonier.org/learn/articles/safe-and-secure.

89 John Stott, *The Epistles of John* (Grand Rapids: Eerdmans, 1983), 105.

90 C. S. Lewis, *Letters to an American Lady* (Grand Rapids: Eerdmans Publishing, 1967).

91 John MacArthur, *The Glory of Heaven* (Wheaton: Crossway Book 1996), 55–56.

92 Paul Tournier, *A Place for You* (New York: Harper and Row, 1968), 9.

93 MacArthur, *The Glory of Heaven,* 142.

94 John Stott, *Christ the Liberator* (Downers Grove: IVP, 1971), 32.

95 Stott, *Christ the Liberator,* 34.

96 Stott, *Christ the Liberator,* 34.